STARTER

STUDENT'S BOOK

with Workbook Digital Pack

CEFR A1

TH!NK

SECOND EDITION

Herbert Puchta,
Jeff Stranks &
Peter Lewis-Jones

CAMBRIDGE UNIVERSITY PRESS

CONTENTS

PRONUNCIATION	THINK!	SKILLS
/h/ or /w/ in question words	**Values:** Don't stop the music!	**Reading** Website: Crazy about music Dialogue: Favourite artists **Writing** Completing a questionnaire: Personal information **Listening** Radio quiz: One-Minute Challenge
Vowel sounds – adjectives	**Values:** Welcoming someone **Train to THINK:** Categorising	**Reading** Text messages: Hi there! Dialogue: A birthday present **Writing** Text message: Describing feelings and things **Listening** Dialogues: Talking about feelings
TOWARDS A2 Key for Schools practice		
this / that / these / those	**Values:** Families	**Reading** Article: Film stars and their families Dialogue: Anna's family **Writing** Description: Your favourite room **Listening** Monologues: Describing family
Word stress in numbers	**Values:** My town/city **Train to THINK:** Exploring numbers	**Reading** Brochure: Great cities to visit Dialogues: In the shops **Writing** Brochure: A brochure for your town / city **Listening** Dialogues: Asking for directions
TOWARDS A2 Key for Schools practice		
Present simple verbs – third person	**Values:** Better together or better alone?	**Reading** Newsletter: Robotics Club is cool! Quiz: Do you need a tech break? **Writing** Paragraph: Days in your life **Listening** Monologues: Describing electronic gadgets
Long vowel sound /eɪ/	**Values:** Helping a friend **Train to THINK:** Attention to detail	**Reading** Article: A real friend Dialogue: A surprise for Ellie **Writing** Paragraph: Describing a friend **Listening** Dialogue: Friendship symbols
TOWARDS A2 Key for Schools practice		
Long vowel sound /ɔː/	**Values:** The importance of sport	**Reading** Article: Sport wonders! Article: An amazing last four minutes **Writing** Paragraph: My favourite sportsperson **Listening** Phone call: Making arrangements
Intonation – listing items	**Values:** Music **Train to THINK:** Memorising	**Reading** Microblogs: #Musicintheforest Dialogue: An interview with a teenage DJ **Writing** Microblogs: Describing a scene **Listening** Radio programme: Musicians around the world
TOWARDS A2 Key for Schools practice		
Intonation – giving two choices	**Values:** How you eat is important	**Reading** Article: Kitchen kids Menu and dialogue: In a restaurant **Writing** Menu: A meal plan for your friend **Listening** Dialogue: Cooking
Past simple regular verbs	**Values:** Hard work and achievement **Train to THINK:** Sequencing	**Reading** Article: She was the first woman in space Article: Sports achievers **Writing** Proposal: A statue in my town **Listening** Dialogue: A prize-giving at school
TOWARDS A2 Key for Schools practice		
Past simple irregular verbs	**Values:** Animals and us	**Reading** Article: Dolphins to the rescue Article: Extinct animals **Writing** Short text: An extinct animal **Listening** Dialogue: Josh's holiday
Word stress – comparatives	**Values:** Transport and the environment **Train to THINK:** Comparing	**Reading** Article: The great race Article: My favourite journey **Writing** Description: Unusual forms of transport **Listening** Dialogue: At the train station
TOWARDS A2 Key for Schools practice		

WELCOME

The alphabet

1 W.01 **Listen to the alphabet. Then listen again and repeat.**

Aa Bb Cc Dd
Ee Ff Gg Hh
Ii Jj Kk Ll
Mm Nn Oo
Pp Qq Rr Ss
Tt Uu Vv Ww
Xx Yy Zz

2 W.02 **Listen to the sounds and repeat.**

/eɪ/	/iː/	/e/	/aɪ/	/əʊ/	/uː/	/ɑː/
a h j k	b c d e g p t v	f l m n s x z	i y	o	q u w	r

3 SPEAKING **Work in pairs. Spell your name to your partner. Your partner writes your name. Is he/she correct?**

Colours

4 **Write the colours in the correct places in the key.**

black | blue | brown | green | grey | orange
pink | purple | red | ~~white~~ | yellow

Key

0 *white*
1 ______
2 ______
3 ______
4 ______
5 ______
6 ______
7 ______
8 ______
9 ______
10 ______

5 SPEAKING **Work in pairs. What colours can you see around you? Tell your partner.**

A

B

C

D

E

F

G

H

I

J

K

L

M

N

O

P

International words

6 Match the words in the list with the pictures. Write 1–16 in the boxes.

1 airport
2 bus
3 café
4 park
5 football
6 hamburger
7 hotel
8 phone
9 pizza
10 restaurant
11 sandwich
12 T-shirt
13 taxi
14 city
15 tablet
16 wi-fi

7 W.03 Listen, check and repeat.

8 SPEAKING Work in pairs. Choose one of the words in Exercise 6 and spell it to your partner. He/She writes the word. Is he/she correct?

Articles: *a* and *an*

1 Match the sentences in the list with the pictures. Write 1–4 in the boxes.

1 It's a red T-shirt.
2 It's a black and green T-shirt.
3 It's an orange T-shirt.
4 It's a blue T-shirt.

A ☐

B ☐

C ☐

D ☐

2 Write *a* or *an*.

0 ___*an*___ airport
1 __________ Indian restaurant
2 __________ red bus
3 __________ pizza
4 __________ black taxi
5 __________ orange phone
6 __________ American football player
7 __________ internet page

The day

3 Write the words in the list under the pictures.

afternoon | ~~evening~~ | morning | night

___*evening*___

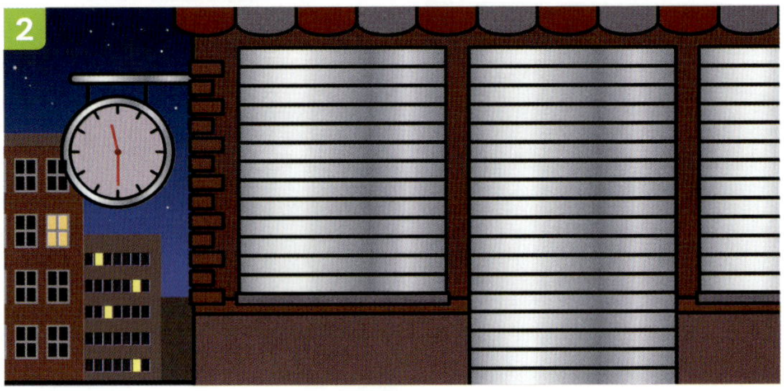

____

____

____

Saying *Hello* and *Goodbye*

4 W.04 **Complete the dialogues with the words in the list. Listen and check.**

Bye | Good | have | Hi | How | morning
night | See you | thanks | ~~this~~

1

Carmen	Hello. My name's Carmen.
Felix	Hi, Carmen. I'm Felix, and [0] ___*this*___ is Isabella.
Isabella	[1] __________, Carmen.
Carmen	Hi, Felix. Hi, Isabella.

2

Harper	[2] __________ afternoon, Mrs Cortez.
Mrs Cortez	Hi, Harper. [3] __________ are you?
Harper	Great, [4] __________. And you?
Mrs Cortez	I'm fine, thanks.

3

Leo	Good [5] __________, Mr Williams.
Mr Williams	Hello, Leo. How are you?
Leo	I'm fine, thank you.
Mr Williams	Good. I'll see you in class.
Leo	[6] __________, Mr Williams.

4

Violet	Bye, Ezra.
Ezra	Bye, Violet. [7] __________ later.
Violet	Yeah, [8] __________ a good day.

5

Lucia	Good [9] __________, Mum.
Mum	Night, Lucia. Sleep well.

Classroom objects

1 **Look at the photos. Do you know these words? If not, ask your teacher: *What's … in English?***

0 *door*

5 ________

1 ________

6 ________

2 ________

7 ________

3 ________

8 ________

4 ________

9 ________

2 W.05 **Write the words in the list under the photos in Exercise 1. Listen, check and repeat.**

board | book | chair | computer | desk
~~door~~ | pen | pencil | projector | window

3 **Do you know any other classroom objects?**

4 SPEAKING **Work in pairs. Point to the photos in Exercise 1. Ask and answer questions.**

What's this in English?

It's a desk.

5 SPEAKING **Work in pairs. Find things in your classroom and say the object and the colour.**

A black pen.

An orange book.

Numbers 0–20

6 W.06 **Look at the numbers 0–20. Listen and repeat.**

0 zero/'oh'
1 one
2 two
3 three
4 four
5 five
6 six
7 seven
8 eight
9 nine
10 ten
11 eleven
12 twelve
13 thirteen
14 fourteen
15 fifteen
16 sixteen
17 seventeen
18 eighteen
19 nineteen
20 twenty

7 SPEAKING **Work in pairs. Choose three numbers from Exercise 6. Tell your partner to write them. Is he/she correct?**

8 W.07 **Listen and write the phone numbers you hear.**

1 ________
3 ________
2 ________
4 ________

9 SPEAKING **Work in pairs. What's your favourite number? Compare.**

Plural nouns

10 **Write the words and the numbers under the pictures.**

0 *two desks*

1 ________

2 ________

3 ________

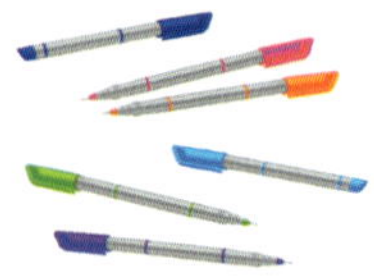

4 ________

5 ________

11 **Match the singular and plural nouns.**

Singular	Plural
0 one man	a three people
1 one woman	b four men
2 one person	c six children
3 one child	d five women

Classroom language

12 W.08 **Listen and number the phrases in the order you hear them. Write 1–10 in the boxes.**

13 W.09 **Listen again and repeat.**

a ☐ Open your books.

b ☐ Listen!

c ☐ Put your hand up.

d ☐ Look at the picture.

e ☐ What does this mean?

f ☐ Sorry, I don't understand.

g ☐ That's right.

h ☐ That's wrong.

i ☐ Close your books.

j ☐ Work with a partner.

Numbers 20–100

1 W.10 **Match the numbers with the words. Listen and check.**

1 20	a fifty
2 30	b eighty
3 40	c ninety
4 50	d seventy
5 60	e one hundred
6 70	f thirty
7 80	g twenty
8 90	h sixty
9 100	i forty

Look

43 = forty-three 85 = eighty-five
77 = seventy-seven

2 W.11 **How do you say these numbers? Listen, check and repeat.**

1 24 2 87 3 33
4 49 5 54 6 62
7 74 8 95

3 **Write the numbers.**

0 23 *twenty-three*
1 47 ____________
2 60 ____________
3 89 ____________
4 34 ____________
5 58 ____________
6 72 ____________
7 91 ____________

Messages

4 W.12 **Read and listen to the message. Complete the message to Alex.**

Alex

Message from Jamie

His house number is [1] ____________ .
The bus number is [2] ____________ .
His phone number is [3] ____________ .

5 W.13 **Now read, listen and complete the message to Molly.**

Molly

Message from Mrs Smith

Her address is [1] ____________ *Main Street, flat number* [2] ____________ .
Her telephone number is [3] ____________ .

Review

6 W.14 **Work in groups. Play the 'first letter' game.**

- Listen to the letter of the alphabet.
- How many examples can you find for each category in the table?
- You get one point for each correct answer. The winner is the group with the most points.

	0 *P*	1 ___	2 ___	3 ___	4 ___	5 ___
Colour	*pink* *purple*					
Actor	*Natalie Portman* *Brad Pitt*					
Classroom object	*pen* *pencil*					
Number (0–20)	*–*					
International word	*pizza* *phone*					
Total points	*8*					

7 Complete the words with the missing vowels. Then complete the table.

0 f *o* *o* t b a l l
1 d _ _ r
2 r _ s t _ _ r _ n t
3 _ r _ n g _
4 p _ n
5 n _ n _
6 c h _ _ r
7 f _ v _
8 y _ l l _ w
9 _ _ r p _ r t
10 g r _ _ n
11 _ _ g h t

International words	Colours	Numbers	Classroom objects
football			

8 Put the dialogues in order. Write 1–4 and 1–3 in the boxes.

1 ☐ **Tom** Great, thanks. And you?
1 **Tom** Good morning, Harry.
☐ **Harry** I'm fine, thanks.
☐ **Harry** Hi, Tom. How are you?

2 ☐ **Amy** Yeah, have a good day.
☐ **Amy** Bye, Paul.
☐ **Paul** Bye, Amy. See you later.

3 ☐ **Dad** Good night, Lars. Sleep well.
☐ **Dad** It's bedtime.
☐ **Lars** OK. Good night, Dad.

9 SPEAKING **Work in pairs. Choose three of the pictures and spell the words for your partner to write. Is he/she correct?**

5

6

7

8

1 ALL TOGETHER

Get THINKING

Watch the video and think: where do you live?

OBJECTIVES

FUNCTIONS: getting to know someone; talking about yourself and others

GRAMMAR: question words; the verb *to be*

VOCABULARY: countries and nationalities; adjectives

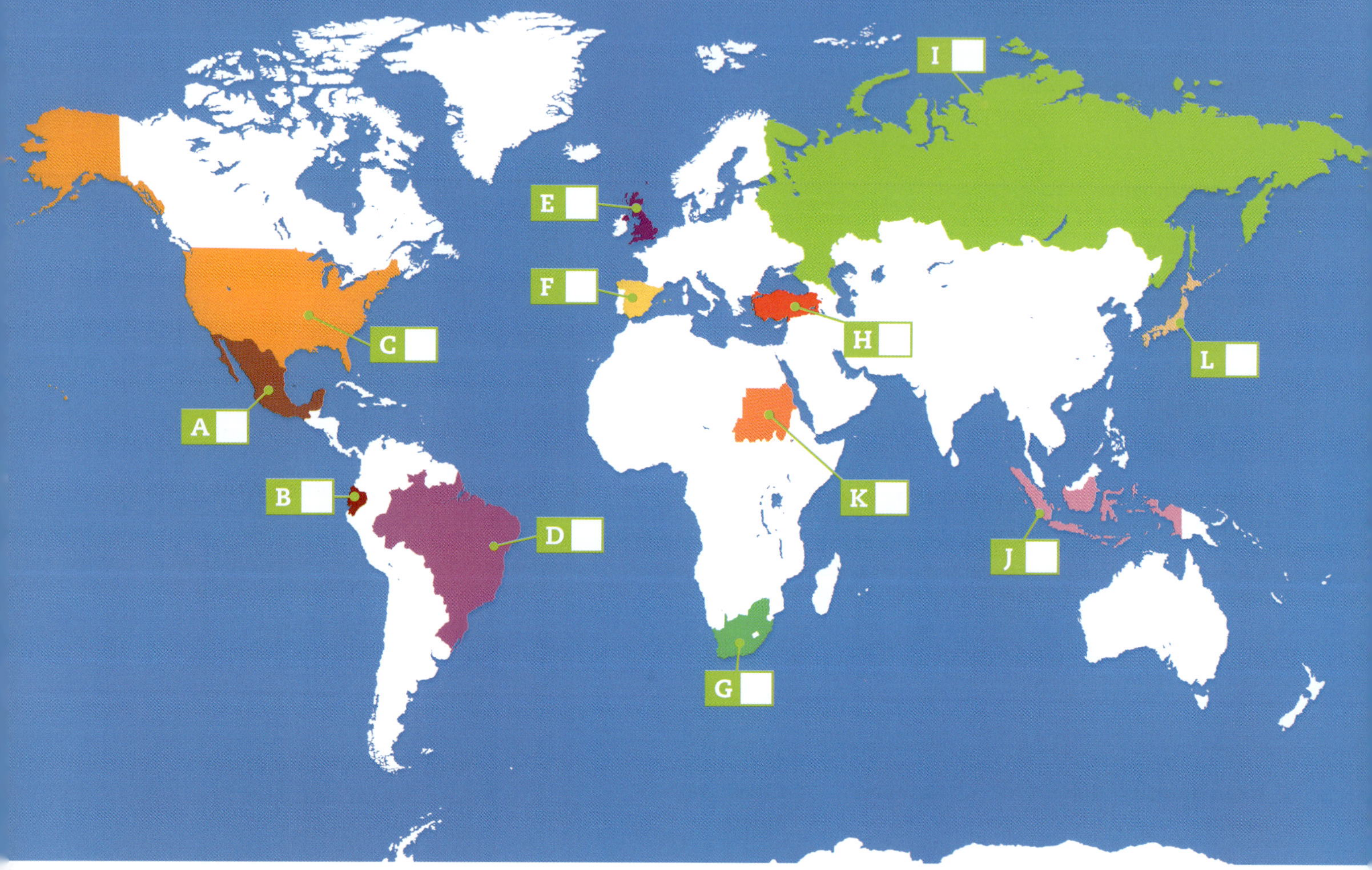

READING

1 **Match the names of the countries with the places on the map. Write 1–12 in the boxes.**

1 Brazil | 2 Ecuador | 3 Indonesia | 4 Japan
5 Mexico | 6 Russia | 7 South Africa | 8 Spain
9 Sudan | 10 Turkey | 11 the UK | 12 the US

2 SPEAKING **Work in pairs. Talk about famous people from different countries.**

Rafael Nadal is from Spain.

3 1.01 **Read and listen to the website. Then choose the correct words.**

0 Cenc is from *Brazil* / *Turkey*.
1 Cenc is *ten* / *11*.
2 Jess is from *Newcastle* / *Manchester*.
3 Bruno Mars is a *singer* / *tennis player*.
4 Flavia is *Brazilian* / *Russian*.
5 Flavia is *11* / *12*.
6 Li Jun is from *Japan* / *Indonesia*.
7 Yuja Wang is a *singer* / *pianist*.

CRAZY ABOUT MUSIC

tell us about your FAVOURITE MUSICIAN!

HOME ABOUT NEWS CONTACT

What's your name?

Cenc.

Where are you from?

I'm Turkish. I'm from a city called Izmir.

How old are you?

I'm ten.

Who's your favourite musician?

Ed Sheeran. He's a singer and a guitar player.

Why is he your favourite musician?

Because he's great!

What's your name?

My name is Jess.

Where are you from?

I'm British. I'm from Newcastle.

How old are you?

I'm 12.

Who's your favourite musician?

Bruno Mars. He's a singer from the US.

Why is he your favourite musician?

Because he's awesome!

What's your name?

I'm Flavia.

Where are you from?

I'm from Brazil. I live in Fortaleza.

How old are you?

I'm 11.

Who are your favourite musicians?

Blackpink. They're a girl group from South Korea.

Why are they your favourite musicians?

Because they're great!

What's your name?

My name is Li Jun.

Where are you from?

I'm from Indonesia. I live in Jakarta.

How old are you?

I'm 11.

Who's your favourite musician?

Yuja Wang. She's a pianist from China.

Why is she your favourite musician?

Because she's cool!

THINK values

Don't stop the music!

4 **Choose a slogan for the website.**

- ☐ One world together.
- ☐ Music is great.
- ☐ Sing, sing, sing!

5 SPEAKING **Work in pairs and compare your answers.**

My slogan is 'One world together.'

Mine is 'Music is great.'

VOCABULARY
Countries and nationalities

1 1.02 **Write the country under the flag. Listen and check.**

~~Brazil~~ | Ecuador | Indonesia | Japan | Mexico | Russia | South Africa | Spain | Sudan | Turkey | the UK | the US

0 *Brazil*

1 ____________

2 ____________

3 ____________

4 ____________

5 ____________

6 ____________

7 ____________

8 ____________

9 ____________

10 ____________

11 ____________

2 Look at Exercise 1. Complete the table with the nationalities of the countries.

-an/-ian	*-ish*	*-ese*
Brazilian	*British*	*Japanese*

3 SPEAKING **Work in pairs. Describe a flag for your partner to guess.**

This flag is yellow, green and blue.

Is it the Brazilian flag?

Yes, it is.

→ workbook page 12

GRAMMAR
Question words

4 Look at the website on page 13. Complete the questions with the words in the list. Then choose the correct words to complete the rule.

How | ~~What~~ | Where | Who | Why

0 *What's* your name?
1 ____________ are you from?
2 ____________ old are you?
3 ____________'s your favourite musician?
4 ____________ is he/she your favourite musician?

RULE: *How, Who, Where, What* and *Why* are [5]*question / because* words.
We often use the word [6]*question / because* to answer a *Why* question.

5 Choose the correct words.

0 *How / Why* old is your best friend? (How circled)
1 *What / Where* is your mother from?
2 *How's / What's* your favourite colour?
3 *Where / Who* is your favourite film star?
4 *Why / Where* is he/she your favourite film star?

6 SPEAKING **Work in pairs. Ask and answer the questions in Exercises 4 and 5.**

What's your name?

My name is Andréa.

→ workbook page 10

PRONUNCIATION
/h/ or /w/ in question words Go to page 120.

LISTENING

7 **Work in pairs. Look at the photos and tick (✓) the correct flag (A or B) for each photo.**

A

☐

1

B

☐

A

☐

2

B

☐

A

☐

3

B

☐

A

☐

4

B

☐

A

☐

5

B

☐

8 1.05 **Listen to a radio quiz called *One-Minute Challenge* and check your answers.**

SPEAKING

9 **Choose things that you like.**

- two colours
- two activities
- one animal

10 **Use your ideas from Exercise 9 to draw a flag.**

11 **Tell your partner about your flag.**

My flag is blue and yellow. They're my favourite colours. Here is a football. It's my favourite sport. Here is music. I love music. Here is a lion. It's my favourite animal.

GRAMMAR
to be

12 **Match sentences a–h with items 1–4. Write the letters in the boxes.**

1 Coco Gauff ☐ ☐
2 paella ☐ ☐
3 Cariocas ☐ ☐
4 Yalitza Aparicio ☐ ☐

a She's American.
b It's Spanish.
c They're Brazilian.
d It's food.
e She's an actor.
f They're from Rio.
g She's a tennis player.
h She's Mexican.

13 **Look at the sentences from the radio quiz. Choose the correct words. Then complete the rule.**

1 I *am* / *are* from Birmingham.
2 You *am* / *are* wrong.
3 It *is* / *are* a Spanish dish.

> **RULE:** The verb ***to be*** changes for different subject pronouns.
> *I **am** American.*
> *You/We/They* [4] ____________ *American.*
> *He/She/It* [5] ____________ *American.*
> We often use contracted forms after pronouns.
> *I am = I'm*
> *You/We/They are = You're / We're / They're*
> *He/She/It is = He's / She's / It's*

Look

Singular	Plural
I	we
you	you
he/she/it	they

14 **Complete the sentences. Use contracted forms where possible.**

0 I *'m* ____________ from New York.
1 She ____________ a famous actor.
2 Liam and Ben ____________ my best friends.
3 We ____________ in Class 2B.
4 You ____________ wrong. Sorry.

→ workbook page 11

READING

1 🔊 1.06 **Read and listen to the dialogue.**
Who knows more about music, Steve or Camila?

Steve Nice T-shirt.
Camila Thank you. It's Ariana Grande.
Steve I know. I'm an Ariana Grande fan, too. So, what's your name?
Camila Camila. And what's your name?
Steve I'm Steve.
Camila Nice to meet you, Steve.
Steve Nice to meet you, too, Camila. Where are you from?
Camila I'm from Spain. I'm from a small town called Teruel.
Steve Spain is a beautiful country.
Camila Yes, it is. Who's your favourite singer?
Steve Umm … er … well, it's that British guy, Shawn Mendes.
Camila Shawn Mendes?
Steve Yes, he's great.
Camila Yes, he is. But he isn't a British singer.
Steve No?
Camila No! He's from Canada!
Steve Oh!
Camila I need to go now. Bye, Steve.
Steve Oh, OK! Bye!

2 **Read the dialogue again. Mark the sentences T (true) or F (false). Then write the correct sentences.**

0 Steve is a Taylor Swift fan. [F]
Steve is an Ariana Grande fan.
1 Camila is Spanish. [ ]
____
2 Camila is from a big town. [ ]
____
3 Shawn Mendes is a singer. [ ]
____
4 Shawn Mendes is from the UK. [ ]
____

3 **Write the questions.**

1 Q ________________
A I'm Steve.
2 Q ________________
A I'm from a small town called Teruel.
3 Q ________________
A Shawn Mendes.

FUNCTIONS
Getting to know someone

4 🔊 1.07 **Put the dialogue in order. Listen and check.**

[ ] **Anna** Nice to meet you, too.
[ ] **Anna** I'm from Rome.
[ ] **Anna** Yes, it is.
[ ] **Anna** I'm Anna.
[1] **Anna** What's your name?
[ ] **Manuel** Nice to meet you, Anna.
[ ] **Manuel** Where are you from, Anna?
[ ] **Manuel** Rome is a beautiful city.
[ ] **Manuel** I'm Manuel. And you?

5 SPEAKING **Work in pairs. Act out the dialogue.**

6 SPEAKING **Work in pairs. Make your own dialogue.**

VOCABULARY
Adjectives

7 1.08 **Write the words in the list under the pictures. Listen and check.**

~~an expensive car~~ | a big hotel | a fast train
a new football | a slow train | a small hotel
a dirty T-shirt | an old football | a cheap car
clean trousers

0 *an expensive car*

1 ____________

2 ____________

3 ____________

4 ____________

5 ____________

6 ____________

7 ____________

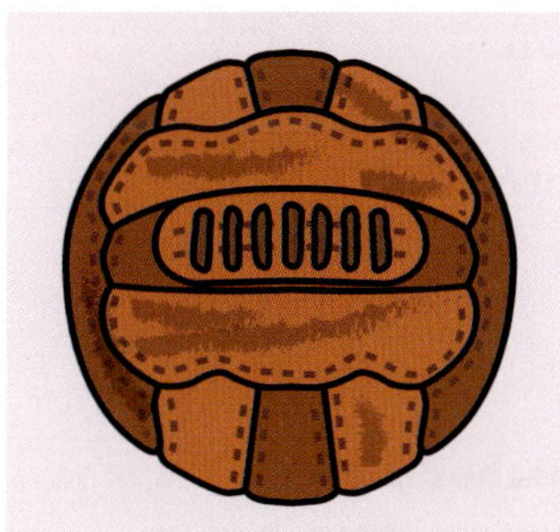

8 ____________

9 ____________

8 **Match the opposites.**

0 new	a slow
1 big	b expensive
2 dirty	c small
3 cheap	d old
4 fast	e clean

9 **Put the words in order.**

0 old / computer / an — *an old computer*
1 a / T-shirt / new — ____________
2 expensive / an / restaurant — ____________
3 car / fast / a — ____________
4 shoes / clean — ____________
5 hotel / cheap / a — ____________

Look

In English, adjectives always stay the same.
new shoes **not** *~~news shoes~~*
green trousers **not** *~~greens trousers~~*

→ workbook page 12

WRITING
Personal information

10 **Look at the questionnaire. Answer the questions about you in full sentences.**

THE LAKES
ENGLISH SUMMER CAMP

We're really excited about your visit next month. Answer the questions about yourself to find the perfect roommate.

What's your name?
____
Where are you from?
____
How old are you?
____
Who's your favourite actor?
____
What's your favourite colour?
____

DEVELOPING SPEAKING

1 **Look at the photo. How many people can you see?**

2 1.09 **Now read and listen to the dialogue. Where is Daniela from?**

Mark: Hi, Tom.
Tom: Hi, Mark. How's it going?
Mark: Great, thanks. Nice skateboard!
Tom: Oh, right. Thanks!
Mark: Who's that?
Tom: That's Daniela.
Mark: Who's she?
Tom: She's new. She's in another class.
Mark: Where's she from?
Tom: I'm not sure. But I think she's Spanish. From Madrid, I think.
Mark: Spanish? Wow! That's awesome.
Tom: I know!
Daniela: Hi, you two. I'm Daniela. I'm new here. I'm from Manchester.
Mark: Manchester? But Tom …
Tom: OK, time to go. See you later, Mark. Bye, Daniela.
Daniela: Bye. Is there a problem?

3 **Read the dialogue again. Mark the sentences T (true) or F (false).**

1 Mark likes Tom's skateboard. ☐
2 Daniela is in Tom's class. ☐
3 Tom thinks Daniela is from Madrid. ☐
4 Daniela is not Spanish. ☐

Phrases for fluency

4 **Find the expressions 1–4 in the dialogue. Who says them? How do you say them in your language?**

1 How's it going? ____________
2 See you later. ____________
3 That's awesome! ____________
4 I know! ____________

5 **Change the underlined expressions. Use an expression from Exercise 4.**

1 A This is my new bicycle.
B Great!
2 A This is a nice computer.
B Yes, it is.
3 Hi, George.
How are you?
4 OK, I'm off now.
Goodbye!

6 **Complete the dialogues with the expressions in Exercise 4.**

0 A Moscow is a city in Russia.
B *I know*!
1 A Hello, Ben!
B ____________?
2 A Look at my new phone.
B ____________!
3 A Goodbye, Mike.
B ____________, Annie.

FUNCTIONS

Talking about yourself and others

KEY LANGUAGE

Questions	Answers
Who's [that/he/she]?	That's / He's / She's [Maria / Ben].

7 **Match the questions with the answers.**

0 Who's that? — b
1 Where's she from?
2 How old are you?
3 Who's your favourite singer?

a She's from Madrid.
b That's Daniela.
c Billie Eilish.
d I'm 11.

8 **Put the words in the correct order to make dialogues.**

1 A that / who's *Who's that?*
B Lucas / that's ____________
A he / from / where's ____________
B the UK / from / he's ____________
2 A they / are / who ____________
B Mario / are / and / they / Alex ____________
A are / from / where / they ____________
B from / they / Mexico / are ____________
3 A Hi, / your / name / what's ____________
B Bea / I'm ____________
A old / you, / how / are / Bea ____________
B 12 / I'm ____________
A favourite / your / actor / who's ____________
B Tom Holland / it's ____________

9 SPEAKING **Work in pairs. Act out the dialogues in Exercise 8. Then make similar dialogues. Use the questions and answers in the Key Language box.**

LIFE COMPETENCIES

Sometimes we are excited about something. We want it to happen now. But we need to wait and be patient.

1 ▶03 **Watch the vlog. Complete the information.**

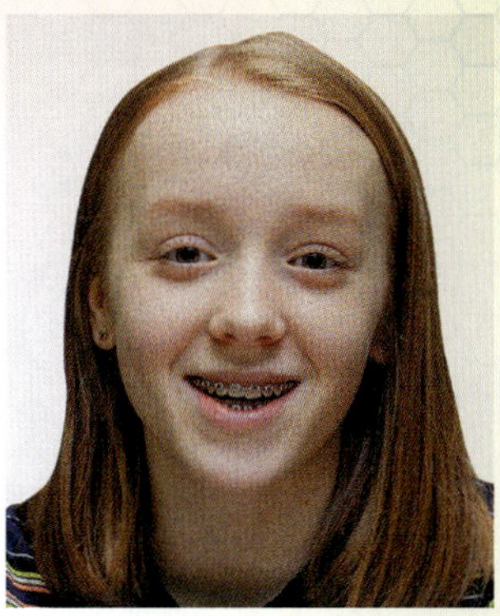

NAME – *Becky*

AGE – ____________

NATIONALITY – ____________

FROM – ____________

FAVOURITE SINGER – ____________

FAVOURITE COLOUR – ____________

BEST FRIEND – ____________

2 ▶03 **Watch the vlog again. Match the sentence halves.**

1 There is a party ☐
2 A trip to have pizza is ☐
3 Becky's birthday is ☐

a next week.
b tomorrow.
c on Saturday.

3 **Read the dialogues. Then match the dialogues with the photos.**

1

Ollie Hi, Mario.
Mario Oh, hi Ollie. I'm excited. Very excited.
Ollie Excited? Why?
Mario It's the big football game tonight.
Ollie When is it?
Mario Eight o'clock. I can't wait.
Ollie That's only three more hours.
Mario I know, but I can't wait!

A ☐

2

Isa Look. This lady in front of us is very slow!
Sara And? What's the problem?
Isa Why is she so slow? I want to get to the cinema!
Sara We have lots of time before our film starts.
Isa Yes! And?
Sara There's lots of time, Isa. Be patient! She's an old lady.

B ☐

Me and my world

4 SPEAKING **Tick (✓) what's true for you. Tell your partner.**

It's difficult to wait …
for my birthday. ☐
for a bus. ☐
for slow people. ☐
for the next school holiday. ☐

TIPS FOR BEING PATIENT

- Remember to wait for other people.
- Ask, 'Why is this person slow?'
- Try to help the person and not get angry.

2 I'M EXCITED

OBJECTIVES

FUNCTIONS: talking about feelings; asking questions; expressing likes and dislikes

GRAMMAR: *to be* (negative, singular and plural); *to be* (questions and short answers); object pronouns

VOCABULARY: adjectives to describe feelings; positive and negative adjectives

Get THINKING

Watch the video and think: when do you feel excited?

READING

1 **Match the phrases in the list with the photos. Write 1–6 in the boxes.**

1 at home | 2 at the cinema
3 at the stadium | 4 at the computer shop
5 at school | 6 at the station

2 SPEAKING **Work in pairs. Act out where you are.**

You're at the stadium.

That's right.

3 2.01 **Read and listen to the text messages. Who isn't happy?**

4 **Read the messages again. Mark the sentences T (true) or F (false).**

0 Lizzie is at home. *F*
1 Lizzie doesn't like the food at the party. ☐
2 Conner is at school. ☐
3 Gemma, Kim and Olivia are hungry. ☐
4 Jud's mum and dad aren't happy. ☐
5 Jud is at the airport. ☐

← **Lizzie**

Hi there, I'm at a party. There are lots of girls and boys here. The food is great. Lots of balloons. There is only one problem. My friends aren't here! I'm sad. 19.45

← **Conner**

I'm at the computer shop with Dad to get my new phone! Dad is angry. The sales assistant isn't here, but the wait isn't a problem for me. I'm not bored. There are lots of cool things here! 10.37

← **Gemma**

I'm at the cinema and I'm so excited! It's the first day of the new Star Wars film. Lots of people are here. Kim and Olivia are with me. We're hungry and thirsty. 🍿 No problem! 12.27

← **Jud**

We're at the station. The train to the airport isn't here. It's late. The plane is at nine tonight and Mum and Dad are a bit worried. I'm not worried. I'm on holiday. No school for six weeks!!!!! 🙂 16.30

THINK values

Welcoming someone

5 Look at the picture and answer the questions.

1 Where is Nathan?
2 How is he?
3 Why isn't Nathan happy?

6 Imagine you are in Nathan's class. What's OK (🙂) or not OK (🙁) to do?

0 talk to Nathan 😀
1 help Nathan
2 smile at Nathan
3 laugh at Nathan
4 not talk to Nathan
5 ask Nathan questions

7 SPEAKING Work in pairs and compare your ideas.

It's OK to smile at Nathan.

It isn't OK to ...

8 SPEAKING Work in pairs. Think of other things you can do to help Nathan.

VOCABULARY
Adjectives to describe feelings

1 2.02 **Match the feelings in the list with the pictures. Write 1–10 in the boxes. Listen and check.**

1 angry | 2 bored | 3 cold | 4 excited
5 hot | 6 hungry | 7 sad | 8 thirsty
9 tired | 10 worried

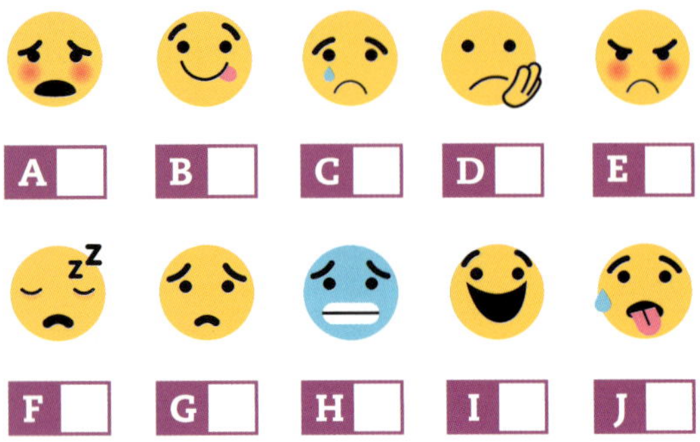

2 Match the pictures with the sentences. Write 1–6 in the boxes.

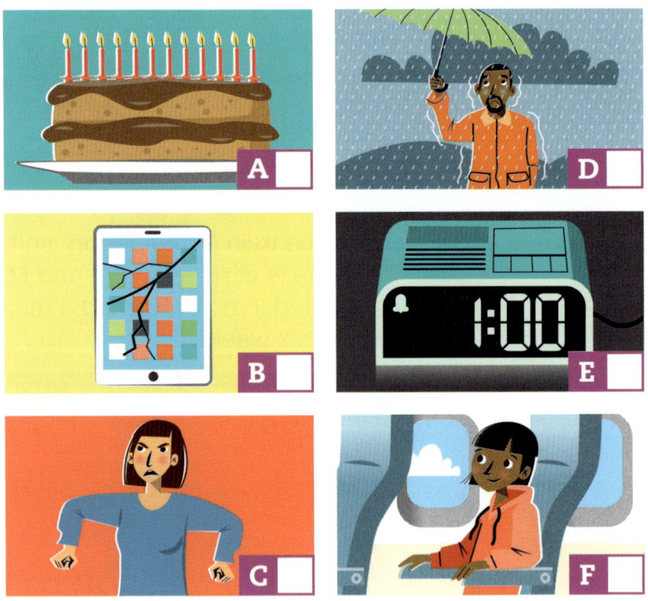

1 It's your birthday.
2 It's one o'clock in the morning.
3 There's a new film on Netflix, but my tablet is broken.
4 The weather is horrible today.
5 Your mum is angry with you.
6 You're on a plane.

3 SPEAKING **Work in pairs. Tell your partner how you would feel in the situations in Exercise 2. Your partner guesses the situation.**

I'm excited.

Number 1?

→ workbook page 20

GRAMMAR
to be (negative, singular and plural)

4 Look again at the text messages on page 21. Complete the sentences. Then complete the rule.

1 My friends ____________ here!
2 The sales assistant ____________ here.

RULE: We form the negative of *to be* with subject + *be* + [3] ____________ .
*I'm **not** sad.* (***am not***)
*You **aren't** sad.* (***are not***)
He/She/It [4] ____________ *sad.* (***is not***)
*We **aren't** sad.* (***are not***)
They [5] ____________ *sad.* (***are not***)

5 Complete the sentences with the correct negative form of *to be*.

1 You ____________ in my team. You're in Mike's team.
2 They ____________ 12 years old. They're 11.
3 No sandwich for me, thanks. I ____________ hungry.
4 Angie's favourite colour is blue. It ____________ green.

6 Complete the sentences with the correct form of *to be*.

1 I ____________ ✗ sad. I ____________ ✓ happy!
2 Danny ____________ ✓ 12. He ____________ ✗ 11.
3 It ____________ ✗ hot. It ____________ ✓ cold!
4 Lucy ____________ ✓ worried. She ____________ ✗ excited.

→ workbook page 18

PRONUNCIATION
Vowel sounds – adjectives Go to page 120.

Train to TH!NK
Categorising

7 Read the words in the list. Put them into three categories. There are four words in each category.

afternoon | angry | bored | evening
excited | grey | morning | night
orange | purple | white | worried

8 SPEAKING **Work in pairs. Compare your categories. Think of a title for each one.**

LISTENING

9 🔊 2.05 **Listen to four dialogues. Match two of the dialogues with the pictures. Write a number (1–4) in the boxes.**

A ☐

B ☐

10 🔊 2.05 **Listen again. Complete the dialogues with *hot*, *worried*, *hungry* and *bored*.**

0 A Is Liam tired?
B No, he isn't. He's *bored* .

1 A Is Lucy thirsty?
B No, she isn't. She's ______ .

2 A Is Tim angry?
B No, he isn't. He's ______ .

3 A Are Eve and Olivia cold?
B No, they aren't. They're ______ .

GRAMMAR

to be (questions and short answers)

11 Look at picture B in Exercise 10. Choose the correct answer. Then complete the rule and the table.

1 A Are you thirsty, Lucy?
B *Yes, I am. / No, I'm not.*

RULE: We form questions with [2]______ + subject.
We form short answers with [3]______ + subject + *to be* (+ *not*).

Question	Short positive answer	Short negative answer
Am I in your team?	Yes, you **are**.	No, you **aren't**.
Are you OK?	Yes, I **am**.	No, **I'm** not.
[4]______ he/she/it OK?	Yes, he/she/it **is**.	No, [7]______ .
Are we in your team?	Yes, we **are**.	No, [8]______ .
[5]______ they OK?	Yes, they [6]______ .	No, they **aren't**.

12 Put the words in order to make questions. Write the answers.

0 African / he / Is / South / ? (yes)
Is he South African? *Yes, he is.*

1 hungry, Josh? / you / Are / ? (no)
______ ______

2 Brazil / they / from / Are / ? (yes)
______ ______

3 you / 12, Eva and Lucia / Are / ? (yes)
______ ______

4 she / Is / tired / ? (no)
______ ______

5 late / I / Am / ? (no)
______ ______

13 Look at the rule again. Complete the dialogues.

1 A *Are* you angry, Keira?
B No, I ______ . I'm just tired.

2 A ______ James and Tim your best friends?
B Yes, they ______ . They ______ in my class at school.

3 A ______ Ms Brown your English teacher?
B No, she ______ . She's my mother's friend.

4 A Am I in your team?
B No, you ______ . You're in Sam's team.

5 A ______ Jules French?
B ______ . He's from Paris.

6 A ______ we late?
B ______ . We're early.

14 SPEAKING **Work in pairs. Ask and answer.**

Is tennis your favourite sport?

Yes, it is.

Are your best friends from the UK?

No, they aren't.

15 SPEAKING **Think of three more questions to ask your partner. Ask and answer.**

→ workbook page 18

READING

1 🔊 2.06 **Read and listen to the dialogue. Then choose the correct option.**

Ruby's birthday is …

a today. ☐
b tomorrow. ☐
c next week. ☐

3 Read the dialogue again and correct the sentences.

0 Ruby is worried.
She isn't worried. She's excited.
1 The Camila Cabello concert is in July.
2 Ruby likes football.
3 Ruby wants a 5 Seconds of Summer T-shirt.
4 There's a new Italian restaurant in town.
5 Ruby likes milk chocolate.

2 Read the dialogue again. Number the photos in the order that Ben talks about them. Write 1–5 in the boxes.

Ruby Hi, Ben, how's it going?
Ben Hey! I'm fine thanks. What about you?
Ruby I'm really excited. It's my birthday.
Ben Your birthday? Today? Isn't it next week?
Ruby No, it's today. So where's my present?
Ben Umm, err. Yes, your present. What do you want?
Ruby I don't know. A surprise?
Ben How about tickets for the Camila Cabello concert in June?
Ruby Wow – that's an expensive present. Camila Cabello? No, I don't like her.
Ben What about a book about football?
Ruby Football? Sorry, I don't like it. I only like tennis.
Ben OK, I know. A 5 Seconds of Summer T-shirt.
Ruby No, thanks. I don't like them any more.
Ben Oh. Can I take you for an ice cream in town? There's a great new Italian ice cream shop.
Ruby Sorry. I don't like ice cream.
Ben This is difficult. No concert, no book, no T-shirt, no ice cream. How about a big bar of chocolate? No? You don't like chocolate?
Ruby Of course I like chocolate.
Ben You do?
Ruby But not milk chocolate. I only like white chocolate.
Ben Only white chocolate. OK.
Ruby Ben. I'm only joking. I don't need a present.
Ben Really?
Ruby Yes, and one more thing …
Ben What's that?
Ruby It isn't my birthday today. It's next week.
Ben Next week! But … Ruby …

A ☐

B ☐

C ☐

D ☐

E ☐

GRAMMAR
Object pronouns

4 **Complete the dialogues with *them*, *it* and *him*. Read the dialogue on page 24 again and check. Then use the words to complete the table.**

Ben How about tickets for the Camila Cabello concert in June?

Ruby Wow – that's an expensive present. Camila Cabello? No, I don't like [1]__________ .

Ben What about a book about football?

Ruby Football? Sorry, I don't like [2]__________ .
I only like tennis.

Ben OK, I know. A 5 Seconds of Summer T-shirt.

Ruby No, thanks. I don't like [3]__________ any more.

Subject	Object
I	me
you	you
he	him
she	[4]__________
it	[5]__________
we	us
they	[6]__________

5 **Complete the dialogues with the correct object pronouns.**

0 A Dad's angry.
B Yes, he isn't very happy with ___*us*___ , Tom.

1 A Do you like BTS?
B No, I don't like __________ .

2 A Do you like Lily James?
B Yes, I like __________ . She's great.

3 A Do you like __________ ?
B Yes, I think you and Peter are great.

4 A Do you like __________ ?
B Yes, I think Jack is funny.

5 A Do you like my new bike?
B Yes, I like __________ .

6 A Bob, I really like __________ .
B I really like you, too, Alice.

6 SPEAKING **Work in pairs. Act out the dialogues from Exercise 5.**

→ workbook page 19

VOCABULARY
Positive and negative adjectives

7 **Look at the words in the list. Write P (positive) or N (negative) in the boxes.**

awful ☐ | bad ☐ | excellent ☐ | exciting ☐
funny ☐ | good ☐ | great ☐ | terrible ☐

8 SPEAKING **Work in pairs. Give one example for each of the things in the list.**

I think Avengers: Endgame is an exciting film.

a a funny film
b an excellent actor/actress
c a bad film
d an exciting computer game
e a great sportsperson
f a terrible singer
g a good book
h an awful actor/actress

→ workbook page 20

FUNCTIONS
Expressing likes and dislikes

9 **Which of these sentences means 'think someone or something is good'? Which means 'think someone or something is bad'?**

1 I don't like Selena Gomez.
2 I like George Ezra.

10 **Put the words in order to make questions.**

A you / like / Little Mix / Do / ?
B you / Dua Lipa / like / Do / ?

11 **Match the answers to the questions in Exercise 10.**

1 No, I don't like them. They're terrible. ☐
2 Yes, I like her. She's great. ☐

12 SPEAKING **Work in pairs. Talk about the films, actors, bands or singers you really like / don't like.**

Do you like Billie Eilish?

Yes, I like her. I think she's great.

Do you like James Bond films?

No, I don't like them. They're terrible.

TH!NK

Masks from around the world

Culture

MASKS FROM AROUND THE WORLD

1 This mask is from Mexico. People wear them for the Day of the Dead Festival on 1st and 2nd November. This festival is popular in many countries in Latin America. People remember family members and friends who are not alive.

2 This is a lion mask from China. In many countries in Asia, there are lion dances. There are always two people in a lion – the mask is on the head of one dancer. The lion dances are very beautiful. Tourists love them.

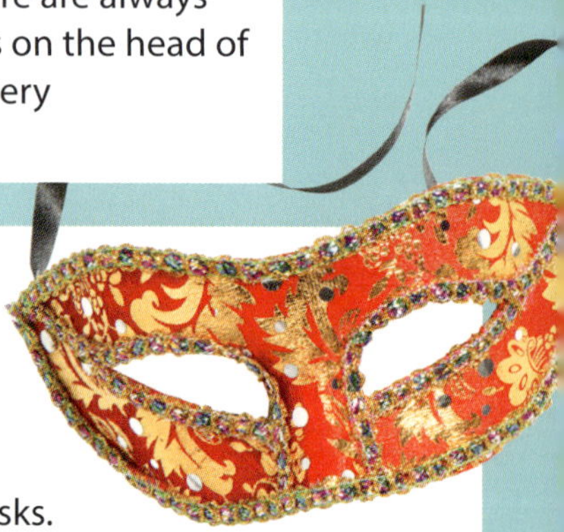

3 Masks are an important part of the carnival in Venice, Italy. There are many different types of carnival masks. For example, the mask in this picture is called the Colombina. Carnival masks are often very beautiful and some are very expensive.

4 This mask is from North America. It's a mask from the First Nations people in Canada. The mask is for the medicine man.

5 These are Halloween masks. Halloween is on 31st October. Children in many countries around the world, for example the US and the UK, wear Halloween masks. They go from house to house and say 'Trick or treat'. People give them sweets ('treats').

1 **Look at the photos on page 26. Find these things.**

a mask from the First Nations people | dancers
flowers | lion | mask | sweets

2 **What feelings can you see in the masks?**

The masks in photo 1 are happy.

3 2.07 **Read and listen to the article. Which countries are the masks from?**

4 **Read the article again. Mark the sentences T (true) or F (false).**

0 The lion dance is from Canada. *F*
1 The North American mask is for a doctor. ☐
2 The Day of the Dead is in November. ☐
3 Halloween is only a holiday in the US and the UK. ☐
4 Colombina is a type of Italian mask. ☐

5 SPEAKING **Which of the masks do you like? Which don't you like? Why? Tell your partner.**

WRITING
Describing feelings and things

1 INPUT **Read the text messages. Write the names under the photos.**

2 **Read the text messages again. Answer the questions.**

1 Where is Clara?
2 Is she happy?
3 Why? / Why not?
4 Where is Henry?
5 Is he happy?
6 Why? / Why not?

3 ANALYSE **How do Clara and Henry ...**

1 start their messages?
2 finish their messages?

4 PLAN **Imagine you want to write a text message to a friend. Think of answers to these questions.**

1 Where are you?
2 Are you happy?
3 Why? / Why not?

5 PRODUCE **Use your answers in Exercise 4 to write a text message (35–50 words) to a friend.**

← Clara

Hi, Sebastian. I'm at school. It's lunchtime and I'm really hungry. But I'm excited. The lunch at school today is excellent! I'm also happy because the sun is out. It's a great day! What about you? Is your day good? Bye.

Saturday, 13.12

← Henry

Hi, Annie. I'm on the train with my family. I'm bored. Three more hours … I've got nothing to do. I'm thirsty, too. How are you? Are you OK? See you soon!

Monday, 10.03

A

____

B

____

TOWARDS A2 Key for Schools

READING AND WRITING

3-option multiple choice cloze

1 Choose the correct answer (A, B or C) for each gap.

Hello. My name's Bryan. I'm [0] *from* South Africa. I live in Johannesburg. I'm 12 [1]______ old. I like music and sport. My favourite sport [2]______ rugby and my favourite player is Bryan Habana (I'm happy [3]______ I have the same name as him!) – but I like football and cricket, too.

I have a sister called Angie. We like music a lot. I like Taylor Swift, but Angie doesn't like [4]______ . Her favourite band is Maroon 5, but I don't like [5]______ much – they're old!

	A	B	C
0	to	from	of
1	how	age	years
2	is	are	am
3	why	because	how
4	she	her	us
5	her	they	them

LISTENING

Gap fill

2 2.08 **You will hear a new girl at school. Write the correct answer in each gap. Write words or numbers.**

New girl at school

Name	0	*Jade Griffin*
Age	1	______
From	2	______
Likes	3	______
Doesn't like	4	______
She is feeling	5	______

TEST YOURSELF

VOCABULARY

1 Complete the sentences with the words in the list. There are two extra words.

awful | Brazil | clean | excited | expensive | hot | hungry | Mexican | old | Spain | South African | thirsty

1 I want a hotdog. I'm ______________________ .
2 She's from Guadalajara. She's ______________________ .
3 Open the window, please. I'm ______________________ !
4 This sandwich is ______________________ . I don't like it!
5 She's ______________________ . I think she's from Johannesburg.
6 I'm 12 and my big sister Mary is 22. She's ______________________ !
7 Are you ______________________ ? OK, here's a glass of water.
8 €450? Oh, it's very ______________________ .
9 São Paulo is a big city in ______________________ .
10 We're on the train to London! We're very ______________________ !

/10

GRAMMAR

2 Complete the sentences with the words in the list.

don't | her | How | it | Where | Why

1 Paul and Magda aren't here. ______________________ are they?
2 This is my new shirt. I really like ______________________ .
3 She's my friend. I like ______________________ a lot.
4 ______________________ old are you?
5 I ______________________ like hamburgers.
6 A ______________________ are you here?
B Because it's a nice place.

3 Find and correct the mistake in each sentence.

1 I not like basketball.
2 What old is your father?
3 Are them from Peru?
4 It aren't an expensive computer.
5 He's the new boy in the class. I like he.
6 What is your favourite footballer?

/12

FUNCTIONAL LANGUAGE

4 Write the missing words.

are | do | don't | from | is (x2) | like | where

1 A Who ______________________ she?
B She's Natasha. She's ______________________ Russia.
2 A ______________________ are they from?
B Brazil. They ______________________ Brazilian.
3 A ______________________ you like Zendaya?
B Yes, I do. She ______________________ a great actress.
4 A I ______________________ like this film. It's awful!
B Oh, really? I ______________________ it. It's funny!

/8

MY SCORE /30

22–30 | 10–21 | 0–9

3 FAMILY TIME

OBJECTIVES

FUNCTIONS:
describing good qualities; talking about family; paying compliments

GRAMMAR:
possessive *'s*; possessive adjectives; *this / that / these / those*

VOCABULARY:
family members; house and furniture

Get THINKING

Watch the video and think: who's in your family?

READING

1 **Match the family members with the photos. Write 1–4 in the boxes.**

1 brother and sister | **2** mother and son
3 father and daughter | **4** husband and wife

2 SPEAKING **Work in pairs. Think of famous examples of the following.**

1 a husband and wife
2 a mother and daughter
3 a father and son
4 sisters
5 brothers

Kit Harington and Rose Leslie are a famous husband and wife.

3 SPEAKING **Look at the photos on the next page. Do you know the people? Talk to a partner.**

4 3.01 **Read and listen to the article. Mark the sentences T (true) or F (false).**

0 Emma Watson is English. *T*
1 Her mother is a lawyer. ☐
2 She's got two brothers and three sisters. ☐
3 Chris Hemsworth's grandmother is Dutch. ☐
4 His wife, Elsa Pataky, is Spanish. ☐
5 He has got three sons. ☐

FILM STARS AND THEIR FAMILIES

EMMA WATSON

Emma Watson is a famous English actress. She is Hermione Granger in the Harry Potter films. Emma's mother and father are lawyers. Her mother's name is Jacqueline Luesby and her father's name is Chris Watson. They live in Oxford, in England.

She's got two sisters. They're twins. They're called Lucy and Nina. She's also got a brother called Toby and a brother called Alex.

Emma is very busy. She's in many films and she is also a UN Goodwill Ambassador.

CHRIS HEMSWORTH AND ELSA PATAKY

Chris Hemsworth is a famous Australian actor. He was born in Melbourne, in 1983, but his grandfather is Dutch and his grandmother is Irish. His wife's name is Elsa Pataky. She is a famous Spanish actress. They have got three children – two sons and a daughter. The two boys are twins. Their names are Sasha and Tristan. Their daughter's name is India Rose.

TH!NK values

Families

5 Complete the sentences with at least one word from the list. Use a dictionary to help you.

friendly | generous | helpful
interested in you | loyal | patient | strict

1 A good brother/sister is ______________ .
2 A good father is ______________ .
3 A good mother is ______________ .
4 A good grandfather/grandmother is ______________ .

6 SPEAKING **Work in pairs and compare your answers.**

I think a good brother or sister is helpful.

I think so, too.

GRAMMAR
Possessive ’s

1 Look at the sentences from the article on page 31. Then complete the rule.

1 Emma’s mother and father are lawyers.
2 His wife’s name is Elsa Pataky.

> **RULE:** We talk about possession with noun + ’s.
> Peter [3] ____________ sister = the sister of Peter

2 Look at the photos and write the correct words with ’s.

my sister

0 *my sister’s phone*

my cousin

3 ____________

William

1 ____________

Hannah

4 ____________

Mrs Smith

2 ____________

my uncle

5 ____________

Look

We use ’s for both possessives and contractions.
Tom’s house is big. (~~The house of Tom is big.~~)
She’s my cousin. (She is my cousin.)

→ workbook page 28

VOCABULARY
Family members

3 3.02 Complete Nick’s family tree with the words in the list. Listen and check.

aunt | brother | cousin | father | grandfather | ~~grandmother~~ | mother | sister | uncle

4 Look again at the article on page 31. Complete the sentences with the words in the list.

daughter | ~~father~~ | husband | son

0 Chris Watson is Emma’s *father* .
1 Lucy is Chris Watson’s ____________ .
2 Elsa Pataky’s ____________ ’s name is Chris Hemsworth.
3 Tristan is Chris Hemsworth’s ____________ .

5 SPEAKING Work in pairs. Write three or four sentences about your family. Tell your partner.

My uncle Antonio is my mother’s brother.

→ workbook page 30

GRAMMAR

Possessive adjectives

6 Look at the article on page 31. Complete the sentences with *His*, *Her* or *Their* and match them with the people. Then complete the table.

1 ____________ mother is a lawyer. ☐
2 ____________ sister is a famous actress. ☐
3 ____________ daughter's name is India Rose. ☐

a Chris Hemsworth
b Emma Watson
c Toby and Alex

Subject	Possessive adjective
I	my
you	your
he	[4] ____________
she	[5] ____________
it	its
we	our
they	[6] ____________

7 Complete the dialogue with the correct possessive adjectives.

Steve Hello. [0] *My* name's Steve. What's [1] ____________ name?
Jane Hi. I'm Jane and this is Renata. She's Brazilian. She's here on holiday with [2] ____________ mother and father.
Steve Hi, Renata.
Renata Hi, Steve. How are you?
Steve Fine, thanks. So, you and [3] ____________ parents are from Brazil?
Renata That's right – we speak Portuguese. It's [4] ____________ first language.
Jane Have you got any brothers or sisters?
Renata No, just me! And you?
Jane Yes, I've got two brothers. [5] ____________ names are Phil and Ricky. They love football! And they love Brazilian football!
Renata Great! My father is a football fan, too – [6] ____________ favourite team is Cruzeiro.

→ workbook page 28

LISTENING

8 🔊 3.03 Listen to three people talking about their family. Write 1–3 in the boxes.

9 🔊 3.03 Listen again. Complete the sentences. Write one word in each space.

1 Ina has got ____________ cousins, but they're in the US. Her brothers are very ____________ to her.
2 Jake's family is very ____________. His ____________ George is his best friend.
3 Maria's family is ____________. She's got ____________ sister, Antonia. Their grandmother is very ____________ and patient.

SPEAKING

10 Complete the 'Me' table. Write the names of four people in your family who are important to you and a word to describe them.

Me

	Name	Adjective
1		
2		
3		
4		

Partner

	Name	Adjective
1		
2		
3		
4		

11 Work in pairs. Ask your partner about their table. Write his/her answers in the 'Partner' table.

12 Tell the class about ...

a your table.
b your partner's table.

READING

1 3.04 **Read and listen to the dialogue and answer the questions.**

1. Where are the two girls?
2. Who is Ellie?

2 **Read the dialogue again and answer the questions.**

1. Is Lucky on the armchair?
2. Is Lucky happy where she is?
3. Are the family happy in the photo?
4. Are Anna's mother and father in the photo?
5. Is the boy Anna's brother?

Lottie So, is [0] *this* your bedroom?

Anna No, it isn't! It's my sister Ellie's bedroom. Do you like it?

Lottie I love [1] ____________ armchair here. And [2] ____________ cushions on the chair are great! But why are we in here?

Anna My cat, Lucky. Look! She's on the bed. She's always there.

Lottie Oh, yes. She's very beautiful. Can we take her to your room?

Anna No, let's leave her here. She's happy here. Come on. Let's go to my room and watch a film.

Lottie Oh, just a minute, Anna. [3] ____________'s a nice photograph. Over there, next to the bed.

Anna Yes, it's me and my family, on holiday in Turkey. We're all very happy!

Lottie Cool. And is [4] ____________ your sister Ellie, there?

Anna Yes, it is. That's Ellie.

Lottie Oh, she's beautiful. And are [5] ____________ two people your parents?

Anna Yes, they are.

Lottie And who is [6] ____________ tall boy next to you? Is it your brother?

Anna No, it isn't. That's my cousin. His name's Max. He lives in Turkey with his mother and father. They're English teachers.

3 3.04 **Complete the dialogue with the words in the list. Listen again and check.**

this (x2) | that (x3) | these | those

GRAMMAR

this / that / these / those

4 **Match the sentences with the pictures. Write 1–4 in the boxes. Then complete the rule.**

1. This is my sister.
2. That's my brother.
3. These are my pens.
4. Those are my friends.

RULE: The words *this* and *that* are [5]*singular / plural*.
The words *these* and *those* are [6]*singular / plural*.
We use *this* and *these* to talk about things that are [7]*near to / far from* us.
We use *that* and *those* to talk about things that are [8]*near to / far from* us.

5 **Look at the pictures in Exercise 4 again. Complete the sentences with *this, that, these* or *those*.**

0. Picture A: Is *this* your phone?
1. Picture B: Are ____________ your books?
2. Picture C: Are ____________ your books?
3. Picture D: Is ____________ your phone?

→ workbook page 29

PRONUNCIATION
this / that / these / those Go to page 120.

VOCABULARY
House and furniture

6 3.07 **Match the rooms in the picture with the words. Write 1–7 in the boxes. Listen and check.**

bathroom ☐
bedroom ☐
garage 1
garden ☐
hall ☐
kitchen ☐
living room ☐

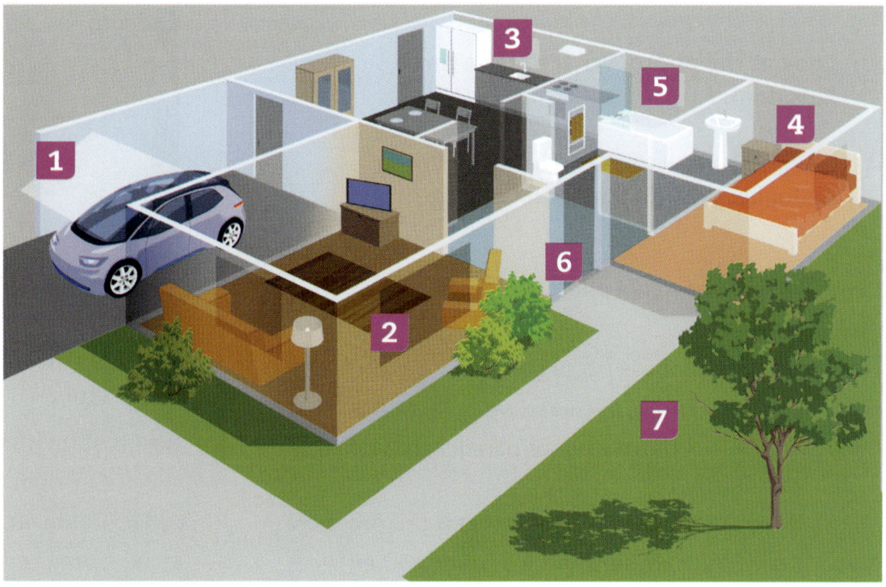

7 3.08 **Match the words with the photos. Write 1–8 in the boxes. Listen and check.**

~~1 armchair~~ | **2** bath | **3** bed | **4** cooker | **5** fridge | **6** shower | **7** sofa | **8** toilet

A ☐

B ☐

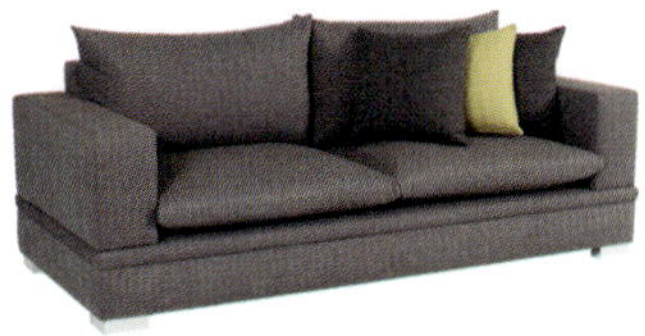
C ☐

D ☐

E ☐

F ☐

G 1

H ☐

8 Complete the table with the words A–H from Exercise 7.

Living room	Kitchen	Bedroom	Bathroom
______	______	______	______
______	______	______	______
______	______	______	______

9 SPEAKING **Work in pairs. Draw an unusual house. Put the furniture in different rooms. Tell your partner about your house.**

The shower is in the kitchen. The bed is in the bathroom.

→ workbook page 30

WRITING
Your favourite room

10 Think about your favourite room in your house. Answer the questions.

- Which room is it?
- Is it big or small?
- What things are in the room?
- What colours are the things in the room?

11 Write a description of your favourite room (about 50 words).

DEVELOPING SPEAKING

1 **Look at the photo. What are the three kids doing?**

2 3.09 **Now read and listen to the dialogue. Why do Paul and Carla go?**

Carla: Wow, what a cool photo!
Abby: Thank you.
Paul: Who are all those people?
Abby: That's my family, of course, on holiday in Spain.
Carla: Ah, OK. So, those are your parents and … that's your brother?
Abby: No, that's my cousin. My brother is this one, here.
Carla: Really? Your cousin looks like your brother!
Abby: I know!
Mum: Excuse me. Hello, everyone.
Paul: Hello.
Mum: Abby, it's almost dinner time.
Abby: Oh, right. Just a minute, Mum.
Carla: Come on, Paul. Let's go.
Abby: Sorry. Let's look at more photos tomorrow.
Paul: Sure. That sounds great. See you, Abby.

3 **Read the dialogue again. Mark the statements T (true) or F (false).**

1 It's a photo from a holiday in Spain. ☐
2 Abby's sister looks like her brother. ☐
3 It's almost time for lunch. ☐
4 They want to look at photos again next week. ☐

Phrases for fluency

4 **Find the expressions 1–4 in the dialogue. Who says them? How do you say them in your language?**

1 Really? ______________
2 Oh, right. ______________
3 Just a minute. ______________
4 Let's go. ______________

5 **Put the sentences in the correct order to make a dialogue.**

☐ **Tom** Just a minute. Let me look at the map.
☐ **Tom** Thanks. Oh. Sally, this is the wrong map.
☐ **Tom** Thanks. Ah, we're on the right road. Let's go.
1 **Sally** Where are we?
☐ **Sally** Really? Oh, right. Sorry. Here's the right map.
☐ **Sally** OK. The map's here. Here you are.

6 **Complete the dialogues with the expressions in Exercise 4.**

1 **A** I love this band. They're fantastic.
B ______________ ? I don't like them.
2 **A** This is a photo of my best friend.
B ______________ . She's very nice.
3 **A** Are you ready?
B ______________ , where's my phone?
Oh, here it is. ______________ .

FUNCTIONS
Paying compliments

KEY LANGUAGE
1 This is / These are [great / cool / awesome / …].
2 He / She / It looks [nice / good / great / …].
3 That's [great / fantastic / cool / …].
4 What a nice [picture / photo / …].
5 I really like …

7 **Complete the dialogues with compliments from the Key Language box.**

1 **A** This photo ______________ .
B Thanks. I like it, too.
A Is that your brother in the photo?
He ______________ .
B Yes, his name's Alex. He's 16.

2 **A** ______________ your shirt.
B Oh, thank you.
A The colours ______________ .
Where's it from?
B It's from my holiday in Turkey.

8 SPEAKING **Act out the dialogues in Exercise 7. Then make new dialogues and act them out, too.**

9 SPEAKING **Tick (✓) the situations when you pay a compliment. Tell a partner what you can say.**

I really like your poster.

1 It's a sunny day. ☐
2 Your friend's sister is in New York on holiday. ☐
3 There is a great poster on your friend's bedroom wall. ☐
4 Your friend has a great new tablet. ☐

LIFE COMPETENCIES

Someone says, ‘goodbye’. You say, ‘goodbye’, too. Someone says, ‘hello’. You say, ‘hello’, too. Someone says, ‘How are you?’ You say, ‘Fine, thanks and you?’ These are examples of having good manners – being polite when people talk to you.

1 ▶09 **Watch the vlog. Who is Ben?**

2 ▶09 **Watch the vlog again. Write the words *thank you*, *sorry* and *please* under the pictures.**

a ____________

b ____________

c ____________

3 **Read the dialogues. Who has good manners? How do you know? Find the polite words and phrases.**

1

Olivia Hi, Suze.
Suze Hello, Olivia. This is my best friend, James.
James Nice to meet you, Olivia.
Olivia Nice to meet you, too, James. I love your shirt.
Suze Really? I don’t like it.
Olivia Oh, I think it’s really cool.
James Thanks, Olivia.
Suze Well, we’re in a hurry. Bye.
James Bye.
Olivia Oh, OK. Goodbye, James. Bye, Suze.

2

Dad Hello, everyone.
Felix Yeah.
Tina Hi, Dad. How are you?
Dad I’m fine, thanks. Are you ready for dinner?
Tina Yes, please, Dad.
Felix I’m really hungry. What is it?
Dad It’s pasta today. Ready in half an hour.
Tina Great! I love pasta! Thanks, Dad.

Me and my world

4 SPEAKING **How do you say these words in your language? When do you use them?**

hello	please
nice to meet you	sorry
thank you / thanks	goodbye

5 SPEAKING **Think about other polite things you say in your language. How important is being polite in your language?**

TIPS FOR HAVING GOOD MANNERS

- When you study a new language, learn the important words for showing good manners.
- Learn when to use them.
- Remember that things might be different in other countries or cultures.

4 CITY LIFE

Get THINKING

Watch the video and think: what do you like to do in a city?

OBJECTIVES

FUNCTIONS: talking about places in a town/city; giving directions; buying in a shop

GRAMMAR: *there is / there are; some / any;* imperatives

VOCABULARY: places in a town/city; prepositions of place; numbers 100+; prices

A

C

B

D

READING

1 **Match the words in the list with the photos. Write 1–4 in the boxes.**

1 a palace | 2 a park | 3 a square | 4 a statue

2 **Work in pairs. Can you name the places in the photographs? Where are they?**

I think it's the Sphinx. It's in Egypt.

3 4.01 **Read and listen to the brochure. Which things from Exercise 1 can you see in Istanbul? Which can you see in Nara?**

4 **Read the brochure again. Mark the sentences T (true) or F (false).**

0 There are only old things to see in Istanbul. *F*
1 Topkapi Palace is in Sultanahmet Square.
2 There are boat trips on the Bosphorus.
3 There is a 15-metre-tall statue in Todai-ji Temple in Nara.
4 The deer can only walk in the park.
5 It is OK to give special food to the deer.

5 SPEAKING **Work in pairs. Ask and answer the questions.**

1 Would you like to go to Istanbul? What would you like to see there?
2 Would you like to go to Nara? What would you like to see there?

GREAT CITIES to visit

Istanbul, Turkey

The wonderful city of Istanbul is a great place to visit. It is an old city, but there are some modern things to see, too. You can visit the beautiful Topkapi Palace and then go to Sultanahmet Square. On one side of the square is the Blue Mosque, and, on the other side, the museum of Hagia Sofia.

Take a boat trip on the Bosphorus – the water between the two sides of the city. Then stop and have coffee – there are many cafés in the city.

Are there any good places to eat? Of course! There are many restaurants, and you can eat great fish for lunch or dinner at Kumkapi Market.

Nara, Japan

Nara is an old city in Japan, about 400 km from Tokyo. It isn't very big – about 400,000 people live there – but it is famous for many things. Many visitors go to see the Todai-ji Temple, a huge wooden building. There is a statue inside. It's over 15 metres tall!

In the city there is a park with hundreds of deer. There aren't any walls in the park, so the deer can walk anywhere in the city. Buy some special food and give it to them – they love it!

TH!NK values

My town/city

6 **Think of your town/city and answer the questions.**

1 What are the most interesting places for you?

2 What are the most interesting places for visitors?

7 SPEAKING **Make one list of interesting places for you and one for visitors. Then compare your answers with a partner.**

The most interesting places in my town/city for me are ...

The most interesting places in my town/city for visitors are ...

8 **Think of a place in your town, city or country to put in a tourist brochure.**

1 What's the name of the place?

2 Why do you want to put it in the tourist brochure?

9 SPEAKING **Work in pairs and compare your ideas.**

I want to put ... in my brochure because it's very old and beautiful.

VOCABULARY
Places in a town/city

1 4.02 **Write the names of the places under the pictures. Listen and check.**

bank | chemist | library | museum | ~~park~~
post office | restaurant | supermarket | train station

0 ______*park*______ 5 ____________________

1 ____________________ 6 ____________________

2 ____________________ 7 ____________________

3 ____________________ 8 ____________________

4 ____________________

2 Complete each sentence with a place from Exercise 1.

0 You buy milk in a *supermarket* .
1 You play football in a ____________ .
2 You eat lunch or dinner in a ____________ .
3 You send packages from a ____________ .
4 You get on a train in a ____________ .
5 You buy medicine in a ____________ .
6 You look at interesting things in a ____________ .
7 You read books in a ____________ .

→ workbook page 38

GRAMMAR
there is / there are

3 Look at the brochure on page 39. Complete the sentences with *is*, *are* and *aren't*. Then complete the table.

1 There ____________ a statue inside.
2 ____________ there any good places to eat?
3 There ____________ any walls in the park.

	Singular nouns	Plural nouns
Positive	There [4]____________	There [6]____________
Negative	There isn't	There [7]____________
Questions	[5]____________ there?	[8]____________ there?

4 Complete the sentences in the positive (+), negative (–) or question form.

0 *There are* six parks in the city. (+)
1 ____________ any cinemas in my town. (–)
2 ____________ a supermarket in your street?
3 ____________ a great restaurant near here. (+)
4 ____________ any people in the café today. (–)
5 ____________ any good museums in this town?

some / any

5 Complete the sentences from the brochure on page 39 with *some* or *any*. Then complete the rule.

1 There aren't ____________ walls in the park.
2 Are there ____________ good places to eat?
3 There are ____________ modern things to see, too.

> RULE: We use ***some*** and ***any*** with plural nouns.
> We use [4]____________ in positive sentences.
> We use [5]____________ in negative sentences and questions.

6 Choose the correct word.

1 There are *some / any* interesting things in the museum.
2 There aren't *some / any* parks in my town.
3 Are there *some / any* good shops here?

7 SPEAKING **Work in pairs. Think of a city, but don't tell your partner! Ask and answer questions.**

Is there a famous palace in your city?

Yes, there is.

→ workbook page 36

VOCABULARY
Prepositions of place

8 Look at the map and complete the sentences with the words in the list.

behind | between | in front of
next to (x2) | ~~on the corner of~~ | opposite

0 The museum is *on the corner of* Green Street and High Street and *next to* the supermarket.
1 The chemist is ______ the library.
2 The cinema is ______ the bank.
3 The sports shop is ______ the park and the post office.
4 The restaurant is ______ the shopping centre.

→ workbook page 38

LISTENING

9 4.03 **Look at the map again. Listen to three people asking for directions. They're starting from the spot labelled 'You are here'. Write the names of the places they want to go to.**

1 ______ 2 ______ 3 ______

10 4.03 **Listen again. Complete the sentences with one word or more.**

1 Go ______ this street, and ______ right.
2 Take the second left into Green Street, and it's ______ .
3 Go ______ the shopping centre, and there's a nice place ______ .

GRAMMAR
Imperatives

11 Complete the examples with *don't*, *go* and *turn*. Then complete the rule.

1 ______ past the supermarket.
2 ______ left.
3 ______ take a bus – it's only two minutes from here.

RULE: To tell someone to do something, you can use the **imperative** – it's the same as the base form of the verb.
To tell someone **not** to do something, use [4] ______ + the base form of the verb.

12 Match the sentence halves.

0 Listen — b
1 Sit
2 Don't open
3 Don't look
4 Turn
5 Go

a the door.
b to me.
c right.
d down, please.
e down the street.
f at the answers.

→ workbook page 37

FUNCTIONS
Giving directions

13 SPEAKING **Work in pairs. Look at the map again. Student A: You're at the restaurant. Student B: Think of another place on the map, but don't say it! Tell Student A how to find you.**

OK, turn right and right again into High Street. Turn right into King Street. It's on the right.

The supermarket?

That's right!

14 SPEAKING **Now change. Student B: You're in the park. Student A: Choose another place on the map and tell Student B how to get there.**

READING

1 4.04 **Read and listen to the dialogues. Where are the people? Write a letter in each box. There are two extra letters.**

A chemist | **B** museum | **C** sports shop | **D** supermarket | **E** train station

1 ☐

Man	Morning. Can I [0] *help you* ?
Girl	Hello. [1] ________ is a ticket?
Man	Are you over 16?
Girl	Yes, I am.
Man	OK, the adult ticket is £15.00. But are you a student?
Girl	Yes, I am. Here's my student card.
Man	OK, that's fine. So it's £7.50, then.
Girl	Great! Here's ten pounds.
Man	OK. And, here's your change – £2.50. Enjoy your visit!
Girl	Thanks – bye!

2 ☐

Man	These are nice. I really like them.
Woman	Yes, they're very nice. Very good for all sports.
Man	And they're comfortable, too. How much [2] ________ ?
Woman	They're £150.
Man	Really? Wow. They're expensive.
Woman	Perhaps, but they're really very, very good trainers. Great for tennis, running … everything!
Man	Yes, you're right. OK, I'll [3] ________ them.
Woman	OK, great. Let's go to the desk to pay.

3 ☐

Woman	Hello. Do you need a bag?
Girl	Um, yes. [4] ________ have one, please?
Woman	Sure. They're 5p each. Wow – that's a lot of potatoes!
Girl	Yes. It's potato salad for dinner tonight!
Woman	Oh, right! So, is that everything?
Girl	Yes, thanks.
Woman	OK, that's £6.95 then. How do you want to pay?
Girl	By card, please.
Woman	Sure. Put it in the machine, please. Thank you. OK, bye – have [5] ________ .
Girl	You, too. Bye!

2 **Read the dialogues again. Complete them with the words and phrases in the list.**

a nice day | are they | Can I | ~~help you~~ | How much | take

3 SPEAKING **Work in pairs. Act out the dialogues.**

VOCABULARY

Numbers 100+

4 4.05 **Match the words with the numbers. Then listen, check and repeat.**

0	130	*d*	**4**	560	☐
1	150	☐	**5**	1,000	☐
2	175	☐	**6**	1,200	☐
3	200	☐	**7**	2,000	☐

a five hundred and sixty
b one thousand two hundred
c two hundred
d one hundred and thirty
e one hundred and seventy-five
f one thousand
g two thousand
h one hundred and fifty

Look

When a number is more than 100, we use the word *and*:
one hundred and twenty
two hundred and sixty-five
We **don't** use the word *and* for numbers 20–99.
twenty-five **NOT** ~~*twenty and five*~~
seventy-three **NOT** ~~*seventy and three*~~

5 4.06 **Listen and write the numbers.**

0 *180* *one hundred and eighty*
1 ______ ________________
2 ______ ________________
3 ______ ________________
4 ______ ________________
5 ______ ________________

→ workbook page 38

PRONUNCIATION
Word stress in numbers Go to page 120.

VOCABULARY
Prices

6 4.09 **Say these prices. Listen and check.**

1 £15.00
2 $25.00
3 €230.00
4 £9.99
5 $21.95
6 €72.50

Look

$ = dollar(s) £ = pound(s) € = euro(s)

£2.50 – In everyday English, we say *two pounds fifty* **not** *two pounds and fifty pence.*

7 4.10 **Listen and look at the prices. Number them in the order you hear them.**

A ☐

D ☐

B ☐

E ☐

C ☐

F ☐

8 SPEAKING **Work in pairs. Ask and answer the questions. Student A: Go to page 127. Student B: Go to page 128.**

→ workbook page 38

FUNCTIONS
Buying in a shop

9 Read these questions and answers. Who says them? Write C (customer) or A (shop assistant).

a Can I help you? ☐
b I'll take them. ☐
c How much are they? ☐
d Here's your change. ☐
e That's £ … , please. ☐
f Have you got … ? ☐

10 Use the questions and answers from Exercise 9 to complete the dialogue. Write a–f.

A Morning. [0] *a*
B Hello. Yes, please. [1] ______ any sports magazines?
A Sure. There's this one here – football – and there's also this one, all kinds of sports.
B Great. [2] ______
A This one is £6.95 and the other one is £6.50.
B OK – [3] ______ both.
A Great. [4] ______ £13.45, ______
B OK, here's £20.00.
A Thank you. [5] ______ , £6.55.
B Thanks. Bye!

11 4.11 **Listen and check your answers. Then act out the dialogue with a partner.**

Train to THINK
Exploring numbers

12 Read, think and write the answers.

Paula, Jack and Ivan go shopping. Paula has got £40. Jack has got £24 and Ivan has got £4. Paula spends £2.80 at the café, £6.60 at the supermarket and £9.60 at the bookshop. Jack spends £6.60 at the post office and £3.40 at the chemist's.

a **At home, Mum asks, 'How much money have you got now?'**
Paula: £ __________
Jack: £ __________
Ivan: £ __________

b **Then Mum says: 'OK, Jack and Paula. Give Ivan some money so that you all have the same!'**
Paula gives Ivan £ __________ .
Jack gives Ivan £ __________ .

TH!NK

Parks around the world

Culture

Parks around the World

1

2

3

4

5

6

A ☐ **Villa Borghese, Rome, Italy**
Villa Borghese is a big public park. There are beautiful gardens, trees and some fountains, too. People also call it 'the park of museums' because there are many interesting museums there.

B ☐ **Golden Gate Park, San Francisco, US**
Everyone knows the Golden Gate Bridge, but did you know that there is a Golden Gate Park in San Francisco, too? It's very big (4.8km long, almost 1km wide) and at one end you can see the sea.

C ☐ **Chapultepec Park, Mexico City, Mexico**
Chapultepec Park is an important green space in this big city. It has a lake and a hill with a castle on it. People in Mexico City love going there.

D ☐ **El Parque del Buen Retiro, Madrid, Spain**
In Madrid there is a very big park called Buen Retiro. There are trees and paths and a lovely rose garden, too. There is also a beautiful glass palace.

E ☐ **The Iguana Park, Guayaquil, Ecuador**
The park's real name is Parque Seminario, but everyone calls it the Iguana Park because it is full of iguanas. The iguanas are very friendly. People go there and feed them.

F ☐ **Mount Faber Park, Singapore**
On a mountain near Singapore, there is a park called Mount Faber. You can get there by cable car. In the park you can walk on a long path, or on an amazing bridge. You get a great view of the city.

1 **Look at the photos on page 44. Find these things and the action.**

bridge | cable car | feed (verb)
fountain | lake | palace

2 4.12 **Read and listen to the article. Match the photos with the texts. Write 1–6 in the boxes.**

3 **Read the article again. Which parks are these sentences about? Write A–F in the boxes.**

0 There is a glass palace here. *D*
1 There are museums inside the park. ☐
2 There is a castle in the park. ☐
3 You can see the city below. ☐
4 You can see animals in this park. ☐
5 This park has the same name as a bridge. ☐

WRITING
A brochure for your town / city

1 INPUT **Read Paul's brochure for his town, Alderley Edge. What things does the town have for visitors?**

2 ANALYSE **Find the adjectives that Paul uses to describe the good things in the town.**

3 PLAN **Plan a brochure for your town/city. Remember to:**

- think of a sentence to introduce your town (name, where it is).
- say what there is in the town.
- give some ideas for things to do there.
- think of a closing sentence.

4 PRODUCE **Use your plan from Exercise 3 to write your brochure (35–50 words).**

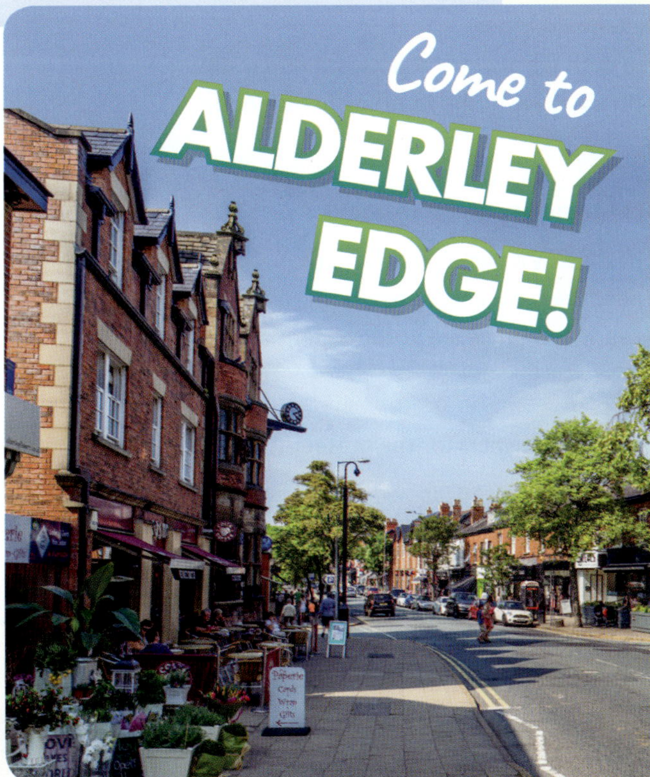

It's a small, pretty town near Manchester – 30 minutes away by train. Alderley Edge has some great shops and lots of lovely cafés.

- Have coffee or a hot drink in one of the cafés.
- Have lunch or dinner – there are some great restaurants!
- Go to the Edge – there is a wonderful view from this hill, and lovely walks, too.
- Go to Manchester – it's not very far, and there are excellent museums and shops there! Or go to Liverpool and see The Beatles Story, a museum about the famous band.

Oh, and some famous football players and managers live in Alderley Edge. Perhaps you'll see someone!

Alderley Edge – a nice place to go to!

TOWARDS A2 Key for Schools

READING AND WRITING

3-option multiple choice

1 **For each question, choose the correct answer.**

1

What does the sign say?

A The sale is for one day.
B Half of the things in the shop are in the sale.
C All the things in the shop are £50.00.

2

What does Amelie say in her message?

A Joanie wants to swim at her school at 4.30.
B Joanie wants to swim after 5.00.
C Joanie wants to swim from 4.30 to 5.00.

3

What does the note say?

A The skateboard is new.
B You can perhaps buy the skateboard for £49.00.
C Don't phone Dave in the morning or afternoon.

4

What does Mum say in her message?

A Jamie has to buy a packet of spaghetti.
B Mum needs two packets of spaghetti.
C Jamie's aunt and uncle are at the supermarket.

5

What is true about tickets for the museum?

A People aged 60 pay £10.00.
B A nine-year-old child pays £12.00.
C One adult with a ten-year-old child pays £30.00.

6

What does the advert say?

A You can get two T-shirts for £8.00.
B You can get three T-shirts for £24.00.
C You can get three T-shirts for £16.00.

Short message

2 **You want to go to the park on Sunday with your English friend Georgia. Write an email to Georgia.**

In the email:

- ask Georgia to go with you
- say what you can do in the park
- say what time you can meet and what time you have to go home.

Write 25 words or more.

VOCABULARY

1 Complete the sentences with the words in the list. There are two extra words.

bathroom | cooker | garage | garden | grandfather | husband
kitchen | library | on the corner of | opposite | sofa | wife

1 Come and sit on the ________________ . Let's watch TV.
2 There's a new fridge in the ________________ . It's really big!
3 There's a ________________ next to the fridge in the kitchen.
4 The cinema is ________________ Allen Street and Green Street.
5 There's a toilet and a shower in our ________________ .
6 She's Mr Graham's ________________ . Her name's Pauline.
7 Our house is nice, but there isn't a ________________ for the car.
8 I love going to the ________________ and choosing books.
9 The supermarket is ________________ the museum.
10 We really love our ________________ . He's eighty-four years old now.

/10

GRAMMAR

2 Complete the sentences with the words in the list.

any | my | some | that | there | those

1 Is ________________ a café here?
2 Hey! Is ________________ your phone? Don't leave it on the desk.
3 How much are ________________ green shoes, please?
4 There aren't ________________ good films on Netflix.
5 Are you hungry? Eat ________________ sandwiches.
6 Please give me back ________________ tablet.

3 Find and correct the mistake in each sentence.

1 There are a really big shopping centre in town.
2 Do you like me new computer?
3 I don't like these table.
4 Doesn't open the window – it's cold in here!
5 That's bike's Jack.
6 Come and play at us house.

/12

FUNCTIONAL LANGUAGE

4 Complete the missing words.

1 **A** Hello. Can I h _ _ _ you?
B Yes, please. H _ _ m _ _ _ are these shoes?
A £32.99.
B Great! I'll t _ _ _ them.

2 **A** Excuse me. W _ _ _ _ is the bank?
B It's in Green Street. It's n _ _ _ to the supermarket.
A In Green Street?
B Yes, walk up here and t _ _ _ left. It's o _ _ _ _ _ _ _ _ a restaurant.

/8

MY SCORE /30

22–30 😊 | 10–21 😐 | 0–9 😣

5 FREE TIME

OBJECTIVES

FUNCTIONS:
talking about habits and activities; talking about technology habits; encouraging someone

GRAMMAR:
present simple; adverbs of frequency; present simple (negative and questions)

VOCABULARY:
free-time activities; gadgets

Get THINKING

Watch the video and think: what do you do in your free time?

A

C

B

D

READING

1 Match the activities in the list with the photos. Write 1–4 in the boxes.

1 build robots | 2 listen to music
3 play sport | 4 play computer games

2 SPEAKING Work in pairs. What activities do you do in your free time? Talk to your partner.

3 Read the newsletter quickly. Which of the activities in Exercise 1 does it talk about?

4 5.01 Read and listen to the newsletter. Mark the sentences T (true) or F (false).

0 Mr Thomas is a Music teacher. T
1 They always make their own robots. ☐
2 They go to a competition every year. ☐
3 They often win the competition. ☐
4 The Robotics Club is only for people at one school. ☐
5 The Robotics Club meets two days a week. ☐

ROBOTICS CLUB IS COOL!

Our school has a Robotics Club and it's brilliant. I know this because I go to it! So, what is a Robotics Club? Easy – it's a club for building robots and I love robots.

Mr Thomas is the club leader. He thinks of things for us to do and helps us build our robots. He's really cool and very kind. He never gets angry with us. He teaches Music (not Design and Technology!), but he just loves everything to do with computers.

We often make our own robots, but we sometimes watch videos of other robots on the internet. When our robot is ready, we use computer programs to make it do things. Every year there is a competition for schools all over the country.

I feel really excited when we show our robots to students from other schools. We never win, but that's not important. The other students like watching our robot move. It feels great.

I love Robotics Club. It's a great place to meet new people. You make so many friends and not just with people from school. Robotics Club is for everyone.

We meet in the school hall every Monday at lunchtime and every Thursday after school. Come and see us – we're always happy to see new people!

TH!NK values

Better together or better alone?

5 **It's good to do some things on your own. But some things are better with friends. Look at the table and tick (✓) the answers that are true for you.**

	Better on my own	Better with friends
make robots		
listen to music		
play sport		
play computer games		
watch TV		
do homework		

6 SPEAKING **Work in pairs and compare your ideas.**

I listen to music on my own.

Me, too!

7 SPEAKING **Think of other activities you like to do on your own and with friends. Tell your partner.**

GRAMMAR
Present simple

1 Look at the newsletter on page 49. Complete the sentences with the correct form of the verbs in the list. Then complete the rule.

like | ~~love~~ | make | meet | think

0 I ___*love*___ robots!
1 He ____________ of things for us to do.
2 The other students ____________ watching our robot move.
3 You ____________ so many friends at Robotics Club.
4 We ____________ in the school hall.

RULE: We add *-s* to the base form of the verb when the subject is *he*, [5]____________ or [6]____________ .
Spelling: If the verb ends in *consonant + -y*, we change the *y* to an *i* and add *-es*.
E.g. *study* → *studies*
If the verb ends in *-ch*, *-sh*, *-ss* or *-x*, we add *-es*.
E.g. *watch* → *watches*

2 Write the correct third-person form of the verbs in the list. Add *-s*, *-es* or *-ies*.

carry | choose | finish | fly | get | go
help | love | miss | study | teach | watch

PRONUNCIATION
Present simple verbs – third person
Go to page 120.

Adverbs of frequency

3 Look at the newsletter on page 49 and complete the sentences. Then complete the rule.

0 He ___*never*___ gets angry with us.
1 We ____________ make our own robots.
2 We ____________ watch videos on the internet.
3 We're ____________ happy to see new people.

RULE:
[4]__________ [5]__________ [6]__________ *always*
0% ————————→ 100%
With the verb *to be* the adverb of frequency usually comes [7]*before / after* the verb.
With other verbs, the adverb of frequency usually comes [8]*before / after* the verb.

→ workbook page 46

VOCABULARY
Free-time activities

4 🔊 5.04 Match the activities in the list with the photos. Write 1–6 in the boxes. Listen and check.

1 play computer games
2 go shopping
3 do homework
4 chat to friends online
5 dance
6 hang out with friends

5 Put the words in order to make sentences.

0 the piano / after school / I / play / always
I always play the piano after school.
1 often / with friends / hang out in / the park / We
2 sad / I / when / I'm / never / dance
3 plays / with her dad / She / sometimes / football
4 in the evening / always / TV / watches / He

6 Complete the sentences with an adverb of frequency so that they are true for you.

1 I ________ play computer games at the weekend.
2 I ________ go shopping with my mum.
3 I ________ do my homework after school.
4 I ________ dance in my bedroom.
5 I ________ chat to my friends online in the morning.

7 SPEAKING Work in pairs. Compare your sentences from Exercise 6. Is anything the same? Then compare your sentences with others in the class.

→ workbook page 48

LISTENING

8 5.05 **Listen to four teenagers talk about their favourite technology. Write the names under the photos.**

~~Ellen~~ | Emilio | Kaia | Ryan

A ____________

C ____________

B ___*Ellen*___

D ____________

9 5.05 **Listen again. Correct the adverb of frequency in each sentence.**

1 Ellen always uses her phone to help her with her homework.
2 The headset is very easy to wear and it sometimes hurts Emilio's head.
3 Ryan's parents often want to use his tablet.
4 Kaia's mum never wants the radio on in the house.

10 SPEAKING **Work in pairs. Tell your partner what technology you use and what you use it for. Use adverbs of frequency.**

I sometimes use my laptop for shopping.

GRAMMAR
Present simple (negative)

11 **Match the sentence halves. Then complete the rule.**

0 I use it for lots of things, but ... [*c*]
1 I don't play games on my TV because ... [ ]
2 It's very thin, and ... [ ]
3 My mum often wants the radio on, but ... [ ]

a it doesn't feel heavy.
b we don't like the same kind of music.
c I don't use it in class.
d they don't feel so real.

RULE: We use *don't* and *doesn't* [4]*before / after* the verb to make negative sentences.
I/you/we/they + [5]__________ + base form
he/she/it + [6]__________ + base form
NOT *don't/doesn't* + present simple form
e.g. ~~He doesn't likes music~~.

12 **Make the sentences negative.**

0 I like Maths.
I don't like Maths.
1 The lesson finishes at two o'clock.
2 My brother helps me with my homework.
3 We go swimming on Sundays.
4 They watch a lot of TV.
5 My aunt lives in Quito.

13 **Complete the sentences with the correct form of the verbs in brackets.**

1 I sometimes ___*play*___ (play) computer games with my mum, but I __________ (not play) them with my dad.
2 My brother __________ (not do) his homework after school. He __________ (do) it in the morning before school.
3 They often __________ (go) to concerts on Friday night, but they __________ (not like) singing.
4 Sofia __________ (not hang out) with her friends after school. She __________ (go) home.
5 I always __________ (listen) to music in the kitchen, but my dad __________ (not like) it.

→ workbook page 47

SPEAKING

14 **Tick (✓) what makes you happy and cross (✗) what doesn't make you happy.**

	Me	My partner
watching TV		
listening to music		
playing computer games		
going shopping		
chatting with friends online		
hanging out with friends		

15 **Work in pairs. Tell each other two things that make you feel happy and two things that don't. Add them to the table. Then tell the class about you and your partner.**

I'm happy when I watch TV.

Carlos isn't happy when he goes shopping.

READING

1 5.06 Read and listen to the quiz from a magazine.

DO YOU NEED A TECH BREAK?

How many hours do you look at a TV, phone, tablet or computer every day?

a less than two
b between two and four
c more than four

Do you check your phone before school?

a never
b sometimes
c always

Do you worry when your phone or tablet has no power?

a never
b sometimes
c always

Do you watch TV before you do your homework?

a never
b sometimes
c always

Does your family ever say that you use your phone too much?

a never
b sometimes
c always

2 SPEAKING Work in pairs. Ask and answer the questions with your partner.

3 Now count your points and read your result. Do you agree with it?

a = 1 point   b = 2 points   c = 3 points

5 to 9	No, you don't need a break! You use it well.
10 to 12	You're not too bad, but be careful!
13 to 15	Yes, you do. You need a break from tech! Do something different!

Grammar rap! ▶14

GRAMMAR

Present simple (questions)

4 Look back at the quiz. Put the words in order to make questions. Then complete the rule.

1 you / homework / do / watch / do / your / TV / before / you / ?
2 school / you / phone / before / your / check / Do / ?

> **RULE:** We use *do* and *does* [3] *before / after* the subject to make questions. We use [4]__________ + I/you/we/they + base form and [5]__________ + he/she/it + base form.
> To answer we use:
> Yes, I/you/we/they **do**. No, I/you/we/they **don't**.
> Yes, he/she/it **does**. No, he/she/it **doesn't**.

5 Choose the correct word.

1 *Do / Does* your best friend play the guitar?
2 *Do / Does* you like ice cream?
3 *Do / Does* your parents play computer games?
4 *Do / Does* your teacher give you a lot of homework?
5 *Do / Does* you hang out with friends at the weekend?

6 Write questions.

0 you / play games with your family?
Do you play games with your family?
1 best friend / live near you?
2 your mum and dad / ask for help with housework?
3 you / like cats?
4 your dad / take you to school?
5 your friends / text you every day?

7 SPEAKING Work in pairs. Ask and answer the questions in Exercises 5 and 6.

Does your best friend play the guitar?

Yes, she does. She sometimes plays for me.

→ workbook page 47

VOCABULARY
Gadgets

8 🔊 5.07 **Match the gadgets in the list with the pictures. Write 1–8 in the boxes. Listen and check.**

1 e-reader | **2** games console | **3** GPS
4 headphones | **5** laptop | **6** smartphone
7 tablet | **8** VR headset

9 SPEAKING **Work in pairs. Tell your partner which of these gadgets you use and don't use every day.**

I use a tablet every day.

I don't use a laptop every day.

10 SPEAKING **Look at the table and make sentences that are true for you.**

I use / don't use a	tablet	to	play games.
	games console		shop.
	VR headset		listen to music.
	smartphone		do homework.
	GPS		read books/magazines.
	laptop		talk to my friends.
	e-reader		watch TV.
	headphones		find out which way to go.

→ workbook page 48

WRITING
Days in your life

11 🔊 5.08 **Complete the days of the week with the missing vowels. Listen and check.**

M <u>o</u> n d <u>a</u> y
T _ _ s d _ y
W _ d n _ s d _ y
T h _ r s d _ y
F r _ d _ y
S _ t _ r d _ y
S _ n d _ y

12 **What do you do or not do on different days? Choose three days and make notes.**

Sunday
- football
- no school

13 **Write about three days of the week. Use your notes from Exercise 12.**

I like Sunday because I always play football and I never go to school. It's a great day.

DEVELOPING SPEAKING

1 Look at the photo. What is wrong with Liz?

2 5.09 Now read and listen to the dialogue. What does Lucy agree to do?

Lucy: Hey, Liz. What's wrong?
Liz: I've got a cold.
Claudio: So? Everyone gets a cold sometimes. What's the problem?
Liz: The problem? The problem is, there's the school concert tomorrow. And I'm the singer!
Claudio: I'm sure you can still sing.
Liz: No way, Claudio! Listen to my voice!
Lucy: She's right. This really is a problem. Oh, Liz, I'm sorry.
Claudio: Don't worry, Liz. We're here to help you.
Lucy: How, Claudio?
Claudio: I don't know!
Liz: Just a minute. I've got an idea. Lucy, you can sing, can't you?
Lucy: A little, Liz. But I can't sing with a band.
Claudio: Oh, come on, Lucy. You can do it. You're a great singer.
Lucy: OK, I'll do it for you, Liz. But this is crazy! OK, what are the songs?
Liz: I'll tell you later. You're the best, Lucy!

3 SPEAKING Read the dialogue again. Answer the questions with a partner.

1 What's tomorrow?
2 Why is this a problem?
3 Who is going to sing in Liz's place?
4 Why does Lucy say: "This is crazy!"?

Phrases for fluency

4 Find the expressions 1–4 in the dialogue. Who says them? How do you say them in your language?

1 What's wrong? ____________
2 No way! ____________
3 I've got an idea. ____________
4 Oh, come on. ____________

5 Put the sentences in the correct order to make a dialogue.

☐ **Molly** Oh, come on, Ben. Please!
☐ **Molly** It's my homework. Can you help me with it?
☐ **Molly** Very funny, Ben.
1 **Molly** Hi, Ben. Listen. There's a problem.
☐ **Ben** No way! I always help you with your homework.
☐ **Ben** Oh? What's wrong?
☐ **Ben** No! But listen – I've got an idea. Ask Mum.

6 Complete the dialogues with the expressions from Exercise 4.

0 A I'm bored.
B Me, too. *I've got an idea.* Let's play football in the park.

1 A Can I talk to you? I've got a problem.
B Oh, no! ____________________

2 A I don't want to come to the party.
B ____________________, Jenny. Parties are great!

3 A Come to the café with me.
B ____________________ I don't like the café.

FUNCTIONS
Encouraging someone

KEY LANGUAGE
You can do it.
Don't worry.
You're great.
I'm / We're here to help you.

7 Put the words in order to make sentences.

1 Maths / great / You're / at
2 worry / test / about / Don't / the
3 can / Of course / you / it / do
4 help / I'm / you / anything / here / with / to

8 Choose one of the pictures and write a dialogue. Use the phrases from the Key Language box.

9 SPEAKING Work in pairs. Act out your dialogues in Exercise 8.

LIFE COMPETENCIES

When our friends or family want to do something very much, we can help and be supportive. We don't try to stop them. We can say things to help them feel good and happy. A good friend is always there for you.

1 ▶15 **Watch the vlog. What is Becky's problem?**

2 ▶15 **Watch the vlog again. Answer the questions.**

1 How old is Julia?
2 What instrument does she play?
3 When is Julia's concert?
4 When does Julia play?
5 What does Becky give her?

3 **Read the dialogues. What problems do Tim and Matt have?**

1 **Tim** This dance is so difficult. I just can't do it.
Luna Of course you can.
Tim No, I can't. I'm not a good dancer.
Luna Yes, you are. You're great. And I'm here to help you, too.
Tim But the show's on Friday. That's only four more days.
Luna OK. Watch me and listen to the music.
Tim Listen to the music?
Luna Yes. Now follow me. Move your arms and legs with the music.
Tim But that's not the same dance.
Luna Yes, but I know another dance. So, come on. Let's practise.

2 **Matt** This homework is too difficult.
Dad What homework?
Matt Maths. I don't understand it!
Dad Let me look. Umm, this is difficult, but I can help.
Matt Can you? I've only got two days to finish it.
Dad No problem.
Matt I'm terrible at Maths, Dad. I really am.
Dad No, you're not. You just need practice. Don't worry. I'm here to help you.
Matt That's very kind, but …
Dad No buts. Let me sit down. Now where's my coffee?
Matt Here it is. Thanks, Dad. You're the best.

4 SPEAKING **Work in pairs. Ask and answer the questions about the dialogues in Exercise 3 with a partner.**

1 Who is supportive?
2 What do they do?
3 What do they say to be supportive?
4 How do you think Tim and Matt feel after the conversations?

Me and my world

5 **Read about Oliver and Marta. What can you say to them?**

Oliver is in the school play tomorrow. He doesn't think he's very good and he's worried about forgetting what to say and do.

Marta is in the school basketball team. They are in the National School Cup final next week. She is worried. She doesn't have much time to practise.

6 SPEAKING **Think about people you know with problems. How can you support them? Tell your partner.**

TIPS FOR BEING SUPPORTIVE

- **Try and find out when a friend has a problem.**
- **Ask them to talk about the problem and listen to them.**
- **Think about how you can help.**

6 BEST FRIENDS

Get THINKING

Watch the video and think: who are your best friends?

OBJECTIVES

FUNCTIONS: helping a friend; describing people

GRAMMAR: *have / has got* (positive, negative and questions); countable and uncountable nouns

VOCABULARY: parts of the body; describing people

A

B

C

D

E

F

READING

1 Match the things in the list with the photos. Write 1–6 in the boxes.

1 brown eyes | **2** curly hair | **3** a glass of water | **4** a jar of coins | **5** a school canteen | **6** a teacher

2 SPEAKING Work in pairs. Complete the sentences so they are true for you. Tell your partner.

1 My eyes are ____________ .
2 My hair is ____________ .
3 My best friend's eyes are ____________ .
4 My mum's hair is ____________ .

3 6.01 Read and listen to the article. How is Julia different from Jack?

4 Read the article again. Match the sentence halves.

0 Julia is 11 and the girls and boys [*d*]
1 Julia eats lunch [ ]
2 Jack only drinks water [ ]
3 Julia wants to buy a scooter [ ]
4 Julia gives the money in the jar [ ]
5 Because Julia is kind, she [ ]

a to her teacher for Jack.
b makes her friend Jack happy.
c in the school canteen every day.
d in her class really like her.
e because he hasn't got any lunch money.
f with the money in the jar.

A real FRIEND

Julia is 11. She has got curly, brown hair, brown eyes and a big smile. She's got a lot of friends at school. All her classmates like her.

At lunchtime, Julia always goes to the school canteen and buys her lunch. Her friend, Jack, doesn't buy any food. He just drinks a glass of water. Jack does this every day, and Julia is worried.

One day, she asks Jack, 'Are you hungry?'

'Yes,' says Jack.

'But you don't eat at school,' says Julia.

'I haven't got any money for lunch,' says Jack. 'My dad hasn't got a job and my mum's ill. They've got lots of problems. But don't worry about me – I'm OK.'

Julia thinks about this. At home, she's got a big glass jar. It's full of coins. She wants to buy an electric scooter one day. That night, Julia opens the jar, takes the coins and puts them into a bag. Her mum sees her. 'Why are you doing that?' she asks.

'My friend Jack hasn't got any lunch money and I've got some money here. This is for him.'

'That's very kind of you,' says her mum. She feels happy that her daughter wants to do this.

The next day, Julia and her mum go and see her teacher. They tell her about Jack and Julia gives her the money. 'This is for Jack's lunch. Now, he can have lunch every day,' she says.

Julia hasn't got an electric scooter, but she's got a happy friend – Jack!

TH!NK values

Helping a friend

5 **Look at these problems your friend has got. Match them to the ways you can help.**

1 My friend is sad.
2 My friend gets a bad mark in his/her History test.
3 My friend is hungry and has nothing to eat.
4 My friend's computer is broken.

a I help him/her study.
b I make him/her a sandwich.
c I lend him/her my tablet.
d I give him/her a hug.

6 SPEAKING **Work in pairs. Think of more ways to help your friends. Use the problems below, or your own ideas.**

1 My friend has got a problem with another student in the class.
2 My friend's parents are angry with him/her.

Grammar rap! ▶17

GRAMMAR

have / has got (positive and negative)

1 Look at the article on page 57. Choose the correct form of *have got* in the sentences. Then complete the rule and the table.

1 She *'ve got / 's got* a lot of friends at school.
2 I *haven't got / hasn't got* any money for lunch.
3 They *'s got / 've got* lots of problems.

RULE: We use *have / has* (+ *not*) + [4] ____________ to talk about possession.

Positive	Negative
I/you/we/they've got (have got)	I/you/we/they [5] ____________ got (have not got)
he/she/it's got ([6] ____________ got)	he/she/it hasn't got (has not got)

2 Complete the sentences with the correct form of *have got*.

0 This laptop is £700. I *haven't got* the money to buy it.
1 My best friend Tony ____________ any sisters, but he ____________ two brothers.
2 I ____________ a tablet, but I really want one.
3 I ____________ a new smartphone. Here's my new number.
4 James and Anna ____________ a car, but they've got bikes.
5 Lara ____________ a big family. She ____________ three sisters and one brother.

→ workbook page 54

VOCABULARY

Parts of the body

3 6.02 Label the picture with the words in the list. Listen and check.

arm | body | ear | eye | face | foot
hand | leg | mouth | nose

4 SPEAKING Work in pairs. Look at the picture and labels for 30 seconds. Then cover the words. Point to the parts of the body and test your partner.

→ workbook page 56

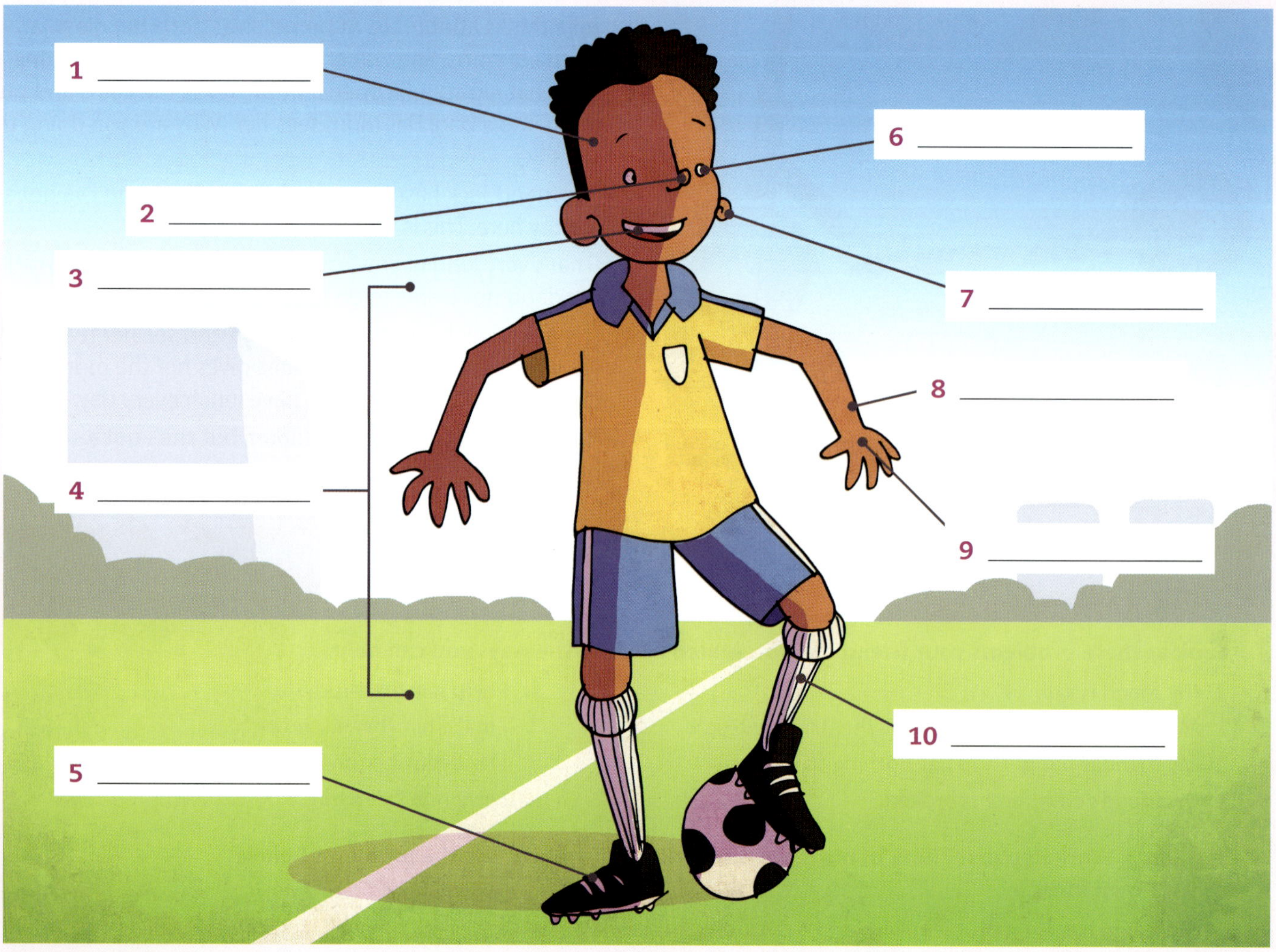

LISTENING

5 Which of these sentences do you agree with?

1 Giving a present to your friend is a great idea.
2 Animals can be our friends.

6 Look at the photos and read the text. Then answer the question.

What other things can you do to show friendship?

7 6.03 **Listen to a conversation in a shop and answer the question.**

What pet has Annie got?

8 6.03 **Listen again. Complete the sentences.**

0 The girl wants to buy a present for her best *friend* .
1 The shop has got a lovely little ____________ rose.
2 Annie's favourite animal is a ____________ .
3 The ____________ is in two pieces.
4 The dolphin is £ ____________ .
5 The girl doesn't buy a necklace. Her friend ____________ one.

GRAMMAR

have / has got (questions)

9 Match the questions and answers. Complete the table.

1 Have you got anything I can buy for my friend? ☐
2 Has your sister got a necklace? ☐
3 Have your grandparents got a dog? ☐

a Yes, she has.
b No, they haven't.
c Yes, I have.

Questions	Short answers
Have I/you/we/they got?	Yes, I/you/we/they have. No, I/you/we/they haven't. (have not)
4 ____________ he/she/it got?	Yes, she/he/it 5 ____________ . No, she/he/it 6 ____________ . (has not)

10 Answer the questions.

1 Have you got your own tablet?
2 Have you got a games console?
3 Have you got a garden?
4 Have you got a big family?
5 Has your best friend got a big family?
6 Have you got a phone with lots of songs on it?

11 SPEAKING **Walk around the classroom. Ask and answer each other the questions in Exercise 10. For each question, find someone with a 'yes' answer and write down their name.**

SHOWING FRIENDSHIP

Many things can show friendship, for example flowers and colours. Some animals can show friendship, too.

A yellow rose

Giving someone a red or pink rose can show that you love them, but giving someone a yellow rose shows that you are their friend.

A heart in two pieces

One friend wears one part of the heart and the other friend wears the other part.

Dolphins

There are many stories about dolphins and people. In these stories, dolphins are often kind and helpful, and show that they are our friends.

Countable and uncountable nouns

12 Complete the table with the words in the list and *a/an* or *some*. Then complete the rule.

~~apple~~ | arm | ~~bikes~~ | chairs | door
friend | ~~fun~~ | hobby | money
pens | time | work

Countable (singular)	Countable (plural)	Uncountable
an apple	*some bikes*	*some fun*

RULE: You **can count** countable nouns: one, two, three, etc. + countable noun (e.g. *two friends, four bikes*).
With singular countable nouns, we use *a* or 1 ____________ .
You **can't count** uncountable nouns (e.g. *time*).
With uncountable nouns and plural countable nouns, we use 2 ____________ .

→ workbook page 54

READING

1 6.04 **Read and listen to the dialogue. Who is the new teacher?**

Ellie Hi, Oliver. Good to see you.

Oliver Hi, Ellie. You look happy. How's it going? How's your first day back at school?

Ellie Not too bad, thanks. We've got this great new teacher. You'd really like him.

Oliver Really? Lucky you. What does he teach?

Ellie Science.

Oliver But you don't like Science.

Ellie I do now. This new teacher's very funny. He makes us all laugh and he makes Science fun. And I understand everything. It's great.

Oliver Really? What does this new teacher look like?

Ellie Well, he's quite tall and he's slim. He's got brown eyes and he wears glasses. He's got short curly hair. It's red like yours.

Oliver He's got red hair?

Ellie Yes, like yours but your hair is straight and his is curly.

Oliver Has he got a beard?

Ellie Yes, he's got a short beard.

Oliver And has he got a moustache?

Ellie Yes … Oh, and he likes sport. He plays rugby and he likes football. He goes to football matches at the weekends with his son. His son's the same age as us.

Oliver Really? And his favourite team is Manchester City.

Ellie Yes, it is. How do you know?

Oliver Is this him walking towards us now?

Ellie Yes, it is.

Oliver That's my dad.

Ellie No way! You're kidding!

2 SPEAKING **Work in pairs. Tick (✓) the picture that shows Oliver's dad. How do you know? Tell a partner.**

1 ☐

2 ☐

3 ☐

3 **Look again at the dialogue and the picture. Write a full description of Oliver's dad.**

VOCABULARY

Describing people (1)

4 **Look at the words in the list. Write them under the correct headings. Some words can go under more than one heading.**

black | blonde | ~~blue~~ | brown | curly | green
grey | long | red | short | straight | wavy

Eye colour	Hair colour	Hair style
blue		

5 SPEAKING **Work in pairs. Use the words in Exercise 4 to describe the people in the photos.**

Zac Efron

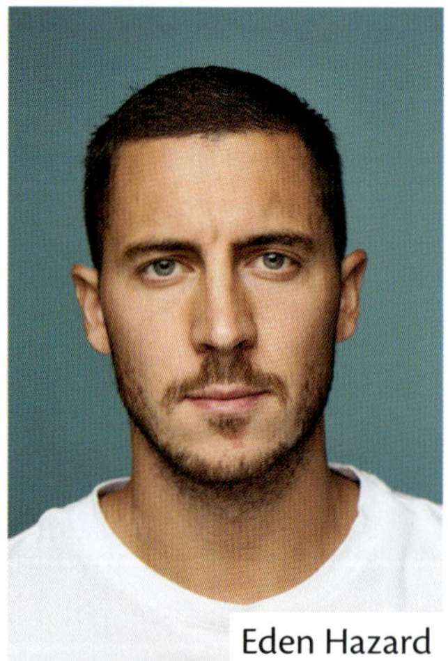

Eden Hazard

Emilia Clarke

Beyoncé

Zac Efron has got …

Beyoncé has got …

→ workbook page 56

PRONUNCIATION
Long vowel sound /eɪ/ Go to page 120.

Describing people (2)

6 6.07 **Match the words in the list with the pictures. Write 1–7 in the boxes. Listen and check.**

1 beard | **2** earring | **3** glasses | **4** moustache | **5** short | **6** smile | **7** tall

A ☐

B ☐

C ☐

D ☐

E ☐

F ☐

G ☐

7 6.08 **Put the words in order to make sentences. Listen and check. Then match each sentence with a picture in Exercise 6.**

0 smile / a / she's / nice / very / got [C]
She's got a very nice smile.

1 She / glasses / wears ☐
______

2 moustache / got / a / He's ☐
______

3 He's / beard / a / got ☐
______

4 got / earring / right / She's / her / ear / an / in ☐
______

5 not short, / she's / quite tall / She's ☐
______

8 6.09 **Complete the dialogue with the missing words. Listen and check.**

A I've got a new friend. His name's Eric.
B What does he look like?
A He's got short brown [0] *hair*, blue [1] e______ and he wears [2] g______.
B Is he tall or [3] s______?
A He isn't very tall.
B Is he nice?
A He's very nice and friendly. He's got a nice [4] s______.

9 SPEAKING **Work in pairs. Act out the dialogue in Exercise 8.**

→ workbook page 56

FUNCTIONS
Describing people

10 Complete the dialogue with answers a–d.

A I'm thinking of a famous footballer.
B What does he look like?
A [0] *d*
B What's he like?
A [1] ______
B Is he French?
A [2] ______
B Is it Paul Pogba?
A [3] ______

a Yes, he is.
b He's really nice.
c Yes, it is.
d He's tall and strong. He's got curly black hair and a nice smile.

11 SPEAKING **Work in pairs. Think of a famous person. Ask and answer questions to guess who he/she is.**

I'm thinking of a famous female singer.

What does she look like?

Train to TH!NK

Attention to detail

12 SPEAKING **Work in pairs. Student A: Go to page 127. Student B: Go to page 128. Describe the people in your picture. Find the six differences.**

13 SPEAKING **Now work with a different partner and compare your answers.**

In picture A, the server has got grey hair. In picture B, ...

TH!NK

Welcoming people around the world

Culture

A

WELCOMING PEOPLE AROUND THE WORLD

How do you say hello to someone you know? Do you smile? Do you touch the other person? Here are some ideas for travellers. This is how people in different countries welcome each other. Do you do different things in your country?

In many countries in Asia, people bow their heads when they meet each other. This shows respect. In India, Nepal and Bangladesh, people bring their hands together in front of their heart and say 'Namaste'.

When you greet a grandmother or grandfather or another older person in Turkey, you kiss their right hand and then place it on your forehead. They do this in the Philippines, too.

The Maori people in New Zealand rub noses together when they meet. This is called the 'hongi'.

In Malaysia, you put your hand on your heart and nod your head. Sometimes you also take the person's hands in your hands first.

In Western countries, many people shake hands when they meet. Sometimes they just smile and say something like 'Hello!' or 'Hi!' In the US and in other countries, some people like using a 'fist bump' to greet another person. Both people make a fist, push their arm forward slowly and touch each other's fists.

In many countries around the world, friends kiss each other on the cheek. In some countries they kiss one cheek, in others they kiss both cheeks and in some they kiss cheeks three times.

H

B

C

D

E

F

G

1 **Look at the photos on page 62. Find these actions.**

bow their heads | bump their fists | kiss
place their right hand on the person's forehead
put their hands together
put their hand on their heart and nod their head
rub noses | shake hands

2 **What do the photos show?**

A people meeting
B people helping people
C people saying thank you

3 6.10 **Read and listen to the article. Say the names of the places in the photos.**

4 **Read the article again. Mark the sentences T (true) or F (false).**

0 In Turkey, you kiss the right hand of a young person. *F*
1 Maori people bring their noses together to say hello. ☐
2 In Malaysia you bring someone's hands to your heart. ☐
3 In Western countries, people never shake hands. ☐
4 In some countries, friends can bump each other's fists to say hello. ☐
5 People only greet others with a kiss in Western countries. ☐
6 In some countries, people kiss three times. ☐

5 SPEAKING **Discuss these questions with a partner.**

1 Which way of welcoming people is your favourite one?
2 How do you welcome people in your country?

WRITING
Describing a friend

1 INPUT **Read the text. Tick (✓) the correct picture of Lily.**

My best friend is called Lily Scott. She's not very tall. She's got long, straight black hair and she wears glasses. She's in my class at school. She's very funny and clever. After school we always walk our dogs in the park and at the weekends we often watch films together. She's a really friendly girl and she's got a very nice smile. She's very popular and everyone likes her. But I'm her best friend!

2 ANALYSE **Read the text again. Complete the notes about Lily.**

Appearance:
hair – 1__________, 2__________
and 3__________
wears 4__________
short

Personality:
friendly – (nice smile!)
5__________ – (has got lots of friends)

3 PLAN **Think about your best friend. Make notes.**

Appearance:
____
____

Personality:
____
____

4 **Answer the questions about your best friend.**

1 What's his/her name?
2 How do you know him/her?
3 Why do you like him/her?
4 What do you do together?

5 PRODUCE **Use your notes from Exercises 3 and 4 to write a short text (about 50 words) about your best friend.**

TOWARDS A2 Key for Schools

READING AND WRITING
3-option multiple choice

1 **For each question, choose the correct answer.**

Tell us about the club you like.
It's the school Lego® club – it's great fun. It's on Tuesdays and Thursdays at lunchtime, for half an hour.

Who organises the club?
The Maths teacher, Mr Jones. We meet in his classroom, 3T. Sometimes we meet outside the classroom.

What does he do?
He's got five big boxes of Lego® bricks. Every week he spends the first ten minutes showing us different ways to build things. Then we practise making things.

Are there competitions?
Yes, there are sometimes competitions. The prize is usually a box of Lego®. But this month there is a competition for schools in the UK to build a Lego® classroom. The winners can go to Legoland®. I hope we win!

1 How many times a week does the club meet?
A two times B three times C four times

2 How long are the meetings?
A 15 minutes B 30 minutes C 60 minutes

3 Where does the Lego® club meet?
A at the library B at the museum C at school

4 Why do they go to the club?
A to learn to build new things B to learn Maths C to be outside

5 What's the prize for the UK schools competition?
A a Lego® model B a box of Lego® C a trip to Legoland®

LISTENING
Matching

2 6.11 **You will hear a boy and a girl talking about some people. Match the people with the things on the right. There are two extra things.**

0 Helen	D
1 Mrs Brown	
2 Jerry	
3 Sylvia	
4 Mandy	
5 Sam	

A beard
B ears
C eyes
D hair
E glasses
F moustache
G nose
H smile

VOCABULARY

1 Complete the sentences with the words in the list. There are two extra words.

beard | curly | dance | do | VR headset | eyes | glasses | go | headphones | necklace | out | short

1 No, I can't go out. I need to ______________________ my homework.
2 I always use ______________________ when I listen to music at home.
3 She's got a silver dolphin on her ______________________ .
4 It's OK music, but you can't ______________________ to it.
5 My eyes aren't very good. That's why I wear ______________________ .
6 Let's ______________________ shopping tomorrow afternoon.
7 He's got a big black ______________________ and a moustache.
8 I like her hair. It's long and ______________________ .
9 He's got really nice blue ______________________ .
10 I want to go and hang ______________________ with my friends this evening.

/10

GRAMMAR

2 Put the words in order to make sentences or questions.

1 like / shopping / She / doesn't ______________________
2 never / They / to / listen / rock music ______________________
3 many / got / You / computer games / haven't ______________________
4 She / money / got / has / lots of ______________________
5 always / I / late / to school / get ______________________
6 lots / got / You / of / have / books ______________________
7 usually / are / tired / on Sunday evenings / We ______________________

3 Find and correct the mistake in each sentence.

1 I go often to the cinema.
2 They listen not to music.
3 He play computer games all the time.
4 Have he got a moustache?
5 She don't do her homework.
6 I've got a work to do tonight.
7 You have got a big family?

/14

FUNCTIONAL LANGUAGE

4 Write the missing words.

doesn't | great | like | look | worry

1 **A** There's a new girl in our class.
B Oh? What is she ______________________ ?
A She's nice. But she ______________________ talk a lot.
B Oh. And what does she ______________________ like?
A She's tall and she's got long black hair.

2 **A** Are you OK?
B No. I can't do this homework.
A Don't ______________________ . I can help you.
B Oh, thanks. You're ______________________ !

/6

MY SCORE /30

22–30 | 10–21 | 0–9

7 LIVING FOR SPORT

Get THINKING

Watch the video and think:
What are your favourite sports?

OBJECTIVES

FUNCTIONS:
talking about abilities; telling the time; talking about routines and dates; making suggestions

GRAMMAR:
can (ability); prepositions of time

VOCABULARY:
sport; telling the time; months and seasons; ordinal numbers

A ☐ ______________

C ☐ ______________

B ☐ ______________

D ☐ ______________

READING

1 **Match the sports in the list with the photos. Write 1–4 in the boxes.**

1 football | 2 rock-climbing | 3 snowboarding | 4 surfing

2 **Look at Exercise 1. In which sports do you do these actions?**

1 kick
2 pull
3 stand
4 run
5 turn
6 swim

3 SPEAKING **Do you do any of the sports in the photos? Tell your partner.**

4 7.01 **Read and listen to the article. Write the names under the photos in Exercise 1.**

Goatee | Maureen | Nikolai | Sloan

5 **Read the article again. Tick (✓) the correct box for each sentence.**

	True	False	doesn't say
0 Nikolai only uses his feet and legs to stop the ball from falling.		✓	
1 Nikolai can do this for more than a day.			
2 Sloan is 14 years old.			
3 Sloan goes very fast on the snowboard.			
4 Maureen was born with no hands.			
5 Maureen doesn't think she is different from other climbers.			
6 Goatee is a young goat.			
7 Goatee can swim very well.			

SPORT WONDERS!

Nikolai Kutsenko, from Ukraine, can do amazing things with a football. He can kick a ball well … but he can also keep the ball in the air with his feet, legs and head. Lots of footballers can do this. But can they do it for 24 hours and 30 minutes without stopping? Nikolai can and it's a world record!

Sloan Henderson, from Utah, is a really good snowboarder – and she's only 14 months old! Her mother and father take her to the mountains, and they put her on a snowboard – and there she goes! Sloan loves to be on the board. People are often surprised when they see her because she doesn't fall over!

American rock-climber **Maureen 'Mo' Beck** was born without her left hand and only part of her left arm, but she can climb really well. She is the winner of two climbing World Championships for disabled athletes, and five national championships. She has her own special way of climbing, but Maureen thinks she is just the same as any other climber.

Goatee can't talk or write, but she can surf! Why is this special? Because Goatee is a goat! She surfs with her owner, Dana McGregor. Dana helps Goatee to stand on the board and together they ride the waves in California. Goatee wears a yellow life-jacket because she can't swim very well! And now there is a children's book about her, too – Dana is the author.

THINK values

The importance of sport

6 **Why do people do sport? Read the reasons below and add two more of your own. Put these reasons in order of importance. Write 1–8 in the boxes.**

- ☐ It's fun.
- ☐ You can make friends.
- ☐ It's good to win.
- ☐ ______________
- ☐ ______________
- ☐ It's easy.
- ☐ It's healthy.
- ☐ It's exciting.

7 SPEAKING **Work in pairs and compare your ideas.**

People do sport because it's fun.

GRAMMAR
can (ability)

1 Look at the article on page 67 and complete the sentences. Then complete the rule and the table.

1 He ___________ kick a ball well.
2 ___________ they do it for 24 hours?
3 She ___________ swim very well.

RULE: We use [4]___________ to talk about ability.
The negative form is [5]___________ .
We don't use *do*/*does* with *can* in questions or negative forms.

Positive	Negative
I/you/we/he/she/it/they can jump.	I/you/we/he/she/it/they [6]___________ (**cannot**) jump.
Questions	**Short answers**
[7]___________ I/you/we/he/she/it/they jump?	Yes, I/you/we/he/she/it/they **can**. No, I/you/we/he/she/it/they **can't**.

2 Write sentences about John with *can* or *can't*.

0 swim ✓
John can swim.
1 sing ✗
2 cook ✓
3 play the piano ✗
4 dance ✗
5 ride a bike ✓

PRONUNCIATION
Long vowel sound /ɔː/ Go to page 121.

3 Look at the activities in the list. Tick (✓) the things you can do.

- ☐ play tennis
- ☐ stand on your head
- ☐ throw a ball 20 metres
- ☐ spell your name in English
- ☐ count to 20 in English
- ☐ say the alphabet in under 10 seconds
- ☐ surf
- ☐ make a cake
- ☐ play the guitar
- ☐ jump really high

4 SPEAKING **Work in pairs. Ask and answer the questions from Exercise 3.**

Can you count to 20 in English?

Yes, I can. 1, 2, 3, 4, …

→ workbook page 64

VOCABULARY
Sport

5 7.04 **Match the words in the list with the photos. Write 1–8 in the boxes. Listen and check.**

1 cycle | 2 dive | 3 do gymnastics | 4 do Taekwondo | 5 play basketball | 6 play volleyball | 7 skateboard | 8 ski

A ☐

E ☐

B ☐

F ☐

C ☐

G ☐

D ☐

H ☐

6 SPEAKING **Work in pairs. Which of these sports can/can't you do? Tell your partner.**

I can ski, but I can't dive.

→ workbook page 66

VOCABULARY
Telling the time

7 7.05 **Match the times in the list with the clocks. Write 1–4 in the boxes. Listen and check.**

1 It's half past eight. | **2** It's three o'clock.
3 It's quarter past ten. | **4** It's quarter to one.

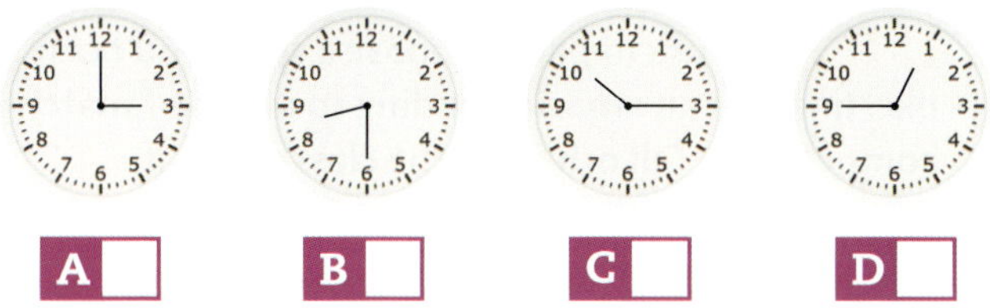

8 SPEAKING **Work in pairs. Write the times under the clocks. Then ask and answer.**

What's the time?

It's quarter past four.

0 *It's quarter past four.*

2 ____________________

1 ____________________

3 ____________________

→ workbook page 66

LISTENING

9 7.06 **Listen to a phone call between Mike and Julia. When do they decide to go cycling?**

10 7.06 **Listen again. Tick (✓) the sports you hear.**

- **a** tennis ☐
- **b** cycling ☐
- **c** rugby ☐
- **d** volleyball ☐
- **e** golf ☐
- **f** Taekwondo ☐

11 7.06 **Listen again. Match the clocks and the sentences. Write 1–8 in the boxes.**

1. The Taekwondo lesson starts at ...
2. The Taekwondo lesson finishes at ...
3. The tennis lesson is at ...
4. The tennis lesson finishes at ...
5. It gets dark at ...
6. The rugby match finishes at ...
7. The rugby match starts at ...
8. The time now is ...

12 Think of four things you do every day. Draw the time that you do them on clocks in your notebook.

13 SPEAKING **Work in pairs. Look at your partner's clocks. Guess what he/she does at each time. Use the things below or your own ideas.**

get up | have breakfast | start school | do sport | do your homework | do your homework | go to bed

Do you get up at half past six?

Do you have breakfast at ...?

SPEAKING

14 Look at the example of a time-cake then draw a time-cake for you.

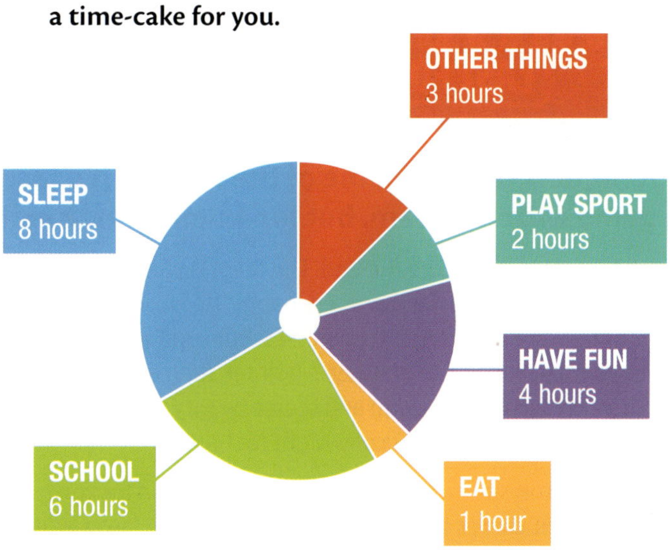

15 Work in pairs. Talk about your time-cake.

1. Are you happy with your time-cake?
2. Would you like to change it? How?

16 Work in pairs. Draw your ideal time-cake. Compare with your partner.

READING

1 SPEAKING **Work in pairs. Discuss these questions.**

1 What do you know about basketball? How long is a game? How do players score points?
2 Which are the best basketball teams?

2 7.07 **Read and listen to the article. Why are the last four minutes amazing?**

3 **Read the first paragraph again. Mark the statements T (true) or F (false).**

1 Jason helps the players in the school team. ☐
2 Jason practises basketball three times a week. ☐
3 Jason plays in his high school basketball team. ☐
4 Jason plays in the first game of the season. ☐

4 **Read the last two paragraphs again. Put the events in order.**

a The coach tells him to go and play. ☐
b Jason scores a 3-point basket. ☐
c The crowd are really happy. ☐
d Jason watches from the bench. *1*
e Jason scores six 3-pointers. ☐
f Jason misses a shot. ☐

5 SPEAKING **Work in pairs. Choose a sport you both like. Imagine an amazing ending to a game / match / competition. Tell others in the class about it.**

Do you like tennis?

Yes, it's my favourite sport. Let's imagine an amazing ending to a tennis game.

AN AMAZING LAST FOUR MINUTES

It's 15th February at Greece Athena High School, New York. Jason McElwain is an 18-year-old student. Jason is autistic. He loves basketball and he helps with the school basketball team. Jason practises hard every day, but he never plays in the team.

Tonight is the last game of the season. It's Jason's last chance to play a game with the team, but for 44 minutes, he sits on the bench and watches.

It's four minutes before the end. The team is winning, so the coach tells Jason to go out and play. The team and the crowd are very happy, because everyone knows Jason and likes him. Jason tries to score a basket, but he misses. But suddenly he hits a 3-point basket. The crowd goes crazy. Jason hits another 3-pointer, then another and another – he hits six 3-pointers (it's a record for the team) and scores twenty points altogether. The team wins, and Jason is a real hero. It's an amazing night for him!

Soon Jason starts to become famous. People in his town know who he is. The US president comes to Jason's town to meet him. Jason writes a book and some people want to make a film about him. He becomes assistant coach to the high school basketball team.

Now Jason works hard to help other autistic people. He travels across the US to help get money for autism research.

VOCABULARY
Months and seasons

6 7.08 **Put the months in the correct order. Write 1–12 in the boxes. Listen and check.**

☐ June	☐ September	☐ April
☐ May	☐ February	☐ December
☐ March	1 January	☐ July
☐ November	☐ August	☐ October

7 In what months are these seasons in your country?

winter

spring

summer

autumn

→ workbook page 66

GRAMMAR
Prepositions of time

8 Read the example sentences and complete the rule with *in*, *at* and *on*.

The football match starts **at** 3 pm.
My birthday is **in** March. It's **in** spring.
The party is **on** Friday.

RULE: With times we use [1]__________ .
For months and seasons we use [2]__________ .
For days of the week we use [3]__________ .

9 7.09 **Do you know when these sporting events are? Guess, then listen and check.**

The World Cup final is usually in June or July.

~~The World Cup final~~	The Winter Olympics
The baseball World Series	Wimbledon
The Summer Olympics	The Tour de France

→ workbook page 65

VOCABULARY
Ordinal numbers

10 Look at the article on page 70. Complete the sentence with the missing date.

It's __________ February at Greece Athena High School, New York.

Look
When we say the date, we usually say **the 7th of** March, but we write **7th** March.

11 7.10 **Match the numbers with the words. Listen, check and repeat.**

1st ☐	9th ☐	**a** sixth	**i** thirtieth
2nd ☐	10th ☐	**b** eleventh	**j** eighth
3rd ☐	11th ☐	**c** thirteenth	**k** thirty-first
4th ☐	12th ☐	**d** third	**l** twelfth
5th ☐	13th ☐	**e** tenth	**m** second
6th ☐	20th ☐	**f** fifth	**n** twentieth
7th ☐	30th ☐	**g** ninth	**o** seventh
8th ☐	31st ☐	**h** first	**p** fourth

12 SPEAKING **Write three important dates for you. Tell your partner about them.**

My sister's birthday is on the 8th of May.

Our school's Sports Day is on the 20th of June.

→ workbook page 66

WRITING
My favourite sportsperson

13 Think of your favourite sportsperson and answer the questions.

1. Who is he/she?
2. Where is he/she from?
3. What sport does he/she do?
4. What sort of things can he/she do?
5. Are there any things he/she can't do?
6. Why do you like him/her?

14 SPEAKING **Work in pairs. Tell your partner about your favourite sportsperson.**

15 Write a short text (50–70 words) about your favourite sportsperson. Use your ideas and answers from Exercises 13 and 14.

DEVELOPING SPEAKING

1 Look at the photo. What sport are Nina and Dave going to do?

2 7.11 Now read and listen to the dialogue. What is the problem?

Nina: Right! Have we got everything? Tennis rackets, balls …?
Dave: Yes, I think so. And we've got some food – sandwiches, fruit and stuff – and some water. So, let's go.
Nina: Just a minute! Oh, no! It's raining! Now what do we do?
Dave: You're right. We can't play outside in the rain.
Nina: Why don't we go to the sports centre in town? They've got an indoor court.
Dave: No, it's always very busy. I'm sure we can't play there today.
Nina: Maybe you're right. It's a bit expensive, too.
Dave: OK, so we can't play today. It's no big deal. We can play tomorrow, perhaps.
Nina: Yes. But I'm a bit sad now.
Dave: Me, too. But what can we do? It's raining, and that's that.
Nina: I know! How about watching some old tennis games on the internet?
Dave: Good idea. I like watching really good players.
Nina: And we can eat our food.
Dave: Let's go and switch the computer on.

3 SPEAKING Read the dialogue again. Answer the questions with a partner.

1 What are Dave and Nina taking with them?
2 Why don't they want to play tennis at the sports centre?
3 How do they feel about not playing tennis?
4 What do they decide to do instead of playing tennis?

Phrases for fluency

4 Find the expressions 1–4 in the dialogue. Who says them? How do you say them in your language?

1 … and stuff __________
2 It's no big deal. __________
3 I'm sure … __________
4 Now what …? __________

5 Put the sentences in the correct order to make a dialogue.

☐ **Paul** You know, books and things. I need them for school. Now what do I do?
☐ **Paul** With no books? I don't think so!
☑ 1 **Paul** I haven't got my school stuff with me.
☐ **Zoe** Oh, it's no big deal. You can go to lessons without books.
☐ **Zoe** What school stuff?
☐ **Zoe** Oh, I'm sure you can. Come on, we're late.

6 Complete the dialogues with the expressions from Exercise 4.

0 A Who is that woman?
B *I'm sure* she's a famous actress. I can't remember her name.

1 A Come to the shops with me.
B I can't. I need to do a lot of work at home, cleaning __________.

2 A My computer is broken.
B But we need the internet! __________ do we do?

3 A I can use my phone. Oh no, I can't find it.
B __________ You can use my phone.

FUNCTIONS
Making suggestions

KEY LANGUAGE
Let's [go to the park].
How about [playing a game]?
Why don't you / we [watch some TV]?

7 Complete the suggestions with the words and phrases from the Key Language box.

1 A I'm bored.
B __________ watching a film?

2 A There's nothing to do.
B __________ go for a walk?

3 A I'm hungry.
B OK. __________ make some sandwiches.

8 SPEAKING Work in pairs. Act out the dialogues in Exercise 7.

9 SPEAKING Make two new dialogues. Choose from these words for speaker A, or use your own ideas.

- thirsty
- tired
- cold
- hot
- sad

LIFE COMPETENCIES

Sometimes we have ideas about what we want to do, but our plans don't always go right. We need to find ways to be happy and positive even when things go wrong.

1 ▶21 **Watch the vlog. Why isn't Ethan happy today?**

2 ▶21 **Watch the vlog again. Tick (✓) the things Ethan wants to do.**

3 **Read the dialogues. Then match the dialogues (1–3) with the photos (A–C).**

1 **Dad** Do you have gymnastics today, Poppy?
Poppy Yes, but my ankle hurts. So I can't go.
Dad Oh no. I know you love gymnastics.
Poppy Yes, I do. But it's no big deal – I can do some exercises with my arms at home.
Dad But that's not the same, is it?
Poppy I know, but I can't do gymnastics today, so I'm happy to do some arm exercises.

2 **Simon** Hey, Agata. How are you?
Agata Not good. We haven't got any electricity. No TV, no internet, nothing. Only my smartphone.
Simon Oh, dear. That's not good. Why not come to my place? We can study together.
Agata Study? I don't want to do that!
Simon OK. So, what do you want to do?
Agata I don't know! Nothing.
Simon Well then, I can't help you. Bye, Agata.

3 **Chloe** Is it a good game?
Jason No! It's 4–0 to the other team. This is awful!
Chloe Oh, I'm sorry about that. But …
Jason But what?
Chloe Well, when the game finishes, we can order pizza!
Jason You're right! What kind of pizza do you want?
Chloe Good for you, Jason! Let's get margherita!

4 SPEAKING **Ask and answer the questions with a partner.**

1 Who is positive from start to end?
2 Who is not positive at the start, but is positive at the end?
3 Who is not positive from start to end?

Me and my world

5 **Tick (✓) the things you sometimes don't feel positive about. Add one of your own.**

You have a lot of homework. ☐
You have a bad cold. ☐
Your brother/sister is annoying you. ☐
______________________ ☐

6 SPEAKING **Work in pairs. Discuss what you can do to feel more positive about the things in Exercise 5.**

TIPS FOR BEING POSITIVE

- Ask yourself: 'Are things really very bad, or just not so good?'
- Think about how you can fix the problem.
- Alone, or with another person, try to think of what you can do to feel OK again.

8 FEEL THE RHYTHM

Get THINKING

Watch the video and think: how important is music in your life?

OBJECTIVES

FUNCTIONS: talking about music and feelings; describing a scene; talking about likes and dislikes

GRAMMAR: present continuous; *like / don't like + -ing*

VOCABULARY: clothes

READING

1 **Match the words in the list with the photos. Write 1–4 in the boxes.**

1 a concert | **2** lights | **3** a singer | **4** a stage

2 SPEAKING **Look at the photos on page 75. Do you know the singer? Do you like concerts? Tell your partner.**

3 SPEAKING **What do you know about Twitter? Do you know of any other microblogs? Tell your partner.**

4 8.01 **Read and listen to the microblog and answer the questions.**

0 How is Lucy feeling at 17.34?
excited
1 Where is Lucy at 18.50?
2 What is Lucy eating at 19.17?
3 What time does the show start?
4 What is Lucy's favourite Jess Glynne song?
5 How is Lucy feeling when she gets home?
6 What time does Lucy go to bed?

#musicintheforest

#Lucybanner

New posts

17.34 I'm leaving home. We're on our way to the station. I'm so excited!

18.05 We're standing on the platform waiting for the train to Delamere Forest.

18.30 We're here. What a fantastic place to see my favourite singer – Jess Glynne – right in the middle of a beautiful forest.

19.17 I'm eating a hot dog. It's very expensive, but it's not very good!

19.57 It's getting dark now. The stage is completely black. A few people are talking, but most people are quiet. We're waiting for Jess. And here she comes. Everyone is cheering. What a noise!

21.45 Jess isn't on stage. Is the show over? No way. We're all shouting 'more'. Why are we shouting? Because we want MORE!!! But don't worry. She's walking back onto the stage.

22.56 We're on the train home. We aren't sitting down. I don't care. There are so many people on the train and everybody's a Jess Glynne fan. We're all singing 'Hold my Hand'. It's my favourite song.

00.00 It's exactly midnight and we're back home. I'm feeling tired but very happy. I'm going straight upstairs to bed.

TH!NK values

Music

5 SPEAKING **Work in pairs. Tick (✓) the places where you listen to music. Tell your partner. How many are the same?**

in my room	☐	on the bus/train	☐
outside	☐	in the shops	☐
at school	☐	another place (where?)	☐

I listen to music in my room, outside and on the bus.

6 **What are your reasons for listening to music? Write 1–3 in the boxes: 3 = a very important reason, 2 = an important reason, 1 = not an important reason.**

☐ It makes me happy.
☐ I can listen with friends.
☐ It's free.
☐ I can forget my problems.
☐ I can dance to it.

7 SPEAKING **Work in pairs and compare your answers.**

Grammar rap!

GRAMMAR
Present continuous

1 **Look at the examples of the present continuous. Find other examples in the microblogs on page 75. Then choose the correct words to complete the rule and the table.**

I'**m leaving** home.
We **aren't sitting** down.
Why **are** we **shouting**?

> **RULE:** We use the present continuous to talk about things that [1]*happen every day / are happening now.* We form the present continuous with the present tense of [2]*to be / to have* and the *-ing* form of the main verb.

Positive	Negative	Question + short answer
I'm (am) listening.	I'm not (am not) listening.	[7]________ I listening? Yes, I [8]________ . No, I'm not.
You/We/They [3]________ (are) listening.	You/We/They aren't (are not) [5]________ .	[9]________ you/we/they listening? Yes, you/we/they are. No, you/we/they [10]________ .
He/She/It [4]________ (is) listening.	He/She/It [6]________ (is not) listening.	[11]________ he/she/it [12]________ ? Yes, he/she/it [13]________ . No, he/she/it isn't.

2 **Look at the pictures. Then write a name to complete the sentences.**

0 *Lucas* is singing.
1 ________ are sitting.
2 ________ is talking on the phone.
3 ________ is leaving.
4 ________ is reading.
5 ________ are dancing.
6 ________ are standing and cheering.
7 ________ is running.
8 ________ is taking a photo.
9 ________ is wearing a skirt.

> **Look**
> Spelling:
> sing – sing**ing** live – liv**ing**
> swim – swimm**ing**

3 **Write the correct *-ing* form of these verbs.**

0 come *coming*
1 take ________
2 get ________
3 shop ________
4 make ________
5 watch ________
6 play ________
7 study ________

4 **Complete the sentences with the verbs from Exercise 3 in the correct form.**

0 **A** Come on, Ruth, we're late!
B OK, Liam, I*'m coming* now!
1 **A** Where's Jane?
B She's in her bedroom. She ________ TV.
2 **A** Is Hamid here?
B No, he isn't. He ________ tennis in the park.
3 **A** Can I talk to Bob, please?
B Sorry, he's at the supermarket. He ________ for food.
4 **A** Let's go home now.
B You're right. It ________ late. Look, it's almost 11 o'clock.
5 **A** Is your dad in the kitchen?
B Yes, he is! He ________ a cake!
6 **A** Where's Paul?
B He ________ the dog for a walk in the street.
7 **A** So, your sister is in Australia.
B That's right. She ________ at a university there.

→ workbook page 72

LISTENING

5 Look at the different musicians in the photos. Say where you think they come from. Choose from the countries in the list.

Brazil | Burundi | China | Indonesia
Mexico | Scotland | Spain

A

C

B

D

6 In which photos can you see these things? Write 1–4 in the boxes.

1 The people are walking and hitting the drums.
2 The men are walking and wearing red and white socks.
3 A man is playing a guitar. He's wearing a big hat.
4 The women are wearing traditional colourful clothes. They are sitting down.

7 8.02 Listen to the radio programme. Which three photos from Exercise 5 do the people talk about?

8 8.02 Listen again. Choose the correct options.

0 Liliana *often* / *sometimes* goes to Mexico.
1 Liliana really likes the *shirts* / *hats* the musicians wear.
2 Lewis thinks that Gamelan sounds *awful* / *beautiful*.
3 The Gamelan musicians wear the *same* / *different* clothes.
4 Jen *likes* / *doesn't usually like* African drumming.
5 The Burundi flag is green, red and *blue* / *white*.

9 Imagine you can watch one of the music performances. Which one do you want to watch?

FUNCTIONS
Describing a scene

10 Match 1–3 with a–c. When we describe a scene, we often use:

1 the present continuous ☐
2 prepositions ☐
3 adjectives ☐

a for colours, sizes, etc.
b to say what people are doing.
c to say where people and things are.

11 Read the text and answer the questions.

1 Which photo from Exercise 5 is this person describing?
2 Underline examples of the language mentioned in Exercise 10 (present continuous, prepositions, adjectives).

There is a group of men. They are all walking in the street. They are carrying a strange instrument under their arms. They are wearing black jackets and green skirts, called kilts. They are also wearing black hats on their heads. They are playing the instruments. They are very serious.

12 SPEAKING Look at the picture. Work in pairs. Describe the scene.

READING

1 Read the interview. Match the interviewer's questions and comments with Danny's answers.

1 What do you do?
2 Thanks, Danny, and good luck.
3 What do you like doing in your free time?
4 Who are you?
5 What do you like wearing?
6 Wow. That's interesting. Can you tell us more?

☐ I'm Danny Boyd. I'm 14 years old and I'm from Luton.

☐ I'm a student at school, and at the weekends I work as a DJ.

☐ I'm a DJ at a local youth club. I play every Saturday from 6pm to 10pm. There's usually about 100 people there. It's great fun. I also sometimes play for big crowds in the park and sometimes on the beach, too.

☐ I love listening to music and finding new songs to play. I like watching films and playing games on my VR headset. But I hate dancing. I know that's a strange thing for a DJ to say. I love watching other people dance, but I never dance myself!

☐ When I'm DJing, I like wearing jeans and a white T-shirt. I also wear a red cap. I don't like wearing shirts and trousers. I wear those every day at school!

☐ Thank you! Why don't you come to one of my shows one day?

2 8.03 **Listen to the interview to check your answers.**

3 Read the dialogue again and complete the sentences.

0 Danny Boyd lives *in Luton.*
1 At the weekends he ______________________
2 He loves music but he hates ______________________
3 He likes wearing ______________________

GRAMMAR

like / don't like + -ing

4 Complete the sentences from the interview. Then complete the rule.

0 I like *watching* films.
1 I don't like __________ shirts and trousers.
2 I love __________ to music.
3 What do you like __________ ?

> **RULE:** We use the verbs *(don't) like* / [4] __________ / *hate* + verb + *-ing* to talk about how we feel about activities.

5 Write *like, don't like, love* and *hate* in the correct places.

😀😀 1 __________
😀 2 __________
☹ 3 __________
☹☹ 4 __________

6 Complete the sentences. Use a verb from Exercise 5 and the correct form of the verb in brackets.

0 I *love watching* sport on TV. 😀😀 (watch)
1 I ______________ to the cinema. ☹ (go)
2 I ______________ early. ☹☹ (get up)
3 My family ______________ to France on holiday. 😀 (go)
4 My best friend ______________ . 😀😀 (run)
5 My parents ______________ . ☹ (dance)
6 ______________ your parents ______________ ? 😀 (cook)
7 ______________ your teacher ______________ homework? 😀 (give)

7 SPEAKING **Look at the sentences in Exercise 6. Which are true for you? Change the ones that are not true for you. Then tell your partner.**

→ workbook page 73

VOCABULARY
Clothes

8 8.04 **Match the clothes in the list with the pictures. Write 1–12 in the boxes. Listen and check.**

1 a coat | 2 a dress | 3 jeans | 4 a jumper
5 a shirt | 6 shoes | 7 shorts | 8 skirt
9 socks | 10 T-shirt | 11 trainers | 12 trousers

9 Look at the pictures in Exercise 8 again. What are the people wearing?

0 Eli is wearing *blue jeans, a white T-shirt and trainers.*
1 Beatrice is wearing ______________________ .
2 Jake ______________________ .
3 Anisa ______________________ .
4 Simon ______________________ .

10 SPEAKING **Work in pairs. Ask and answer the questions.**

1 What clothes do you love wearing? What clothes do you hate wearing?
2 Do you like shopping for clothes? Why or why not?
3 What is your teacher wearing today?
4 Which colour do you love or hate wearing?

I love wearing jeans and trainers, but I hate wearing shoes and trousers.

→ workbook page 74

PRONUNCIATION
Intonation – listing items Go to page 121.

Train to THINK
Memorising

11 Look at the picture for two minutes.

12 SPEAKING **Student A: Turn to page 127. Student B: Turn to page 128. Listen to the questions your partner asks and answer them with short answers. Correct the negative answers.**

TH!NK

Dances around the world

Culture

DANCES AROUND THE WORLD

1 THE TANGO

The Tango is the national dance of Argentina, and every year on 11th December people in Buenos Aires celebrate the Day of the Tango. They do the tango in dance halls, parks and squares all over the city. The dance is usually performed by a man and a woman. The man often wears smart trousers and a shirt. The woman often wears a beautiful dress. The dance is often very interesting to watch.

2 THE WHIRLING DERVISH

The Whirling Dervish is a dance from Turkey. There is a group of twelve men who dance. They wear traditional costumes with big skirts. They often all wear white, but sometimes the skirts are different colours. There is another group of twelve musicians. They play traditional Turkish instruments. As the music plays, the dancers spin around in circles, getting faster and faster. The dance is very popular with tourists.

3 IRISH DANCING

There are lots of Irish dances, but perhaps the most famous one is the 'step dance'. One or more dancers perform the step dance. The dancers only move their legs. They move them very quickly. The top half of the body doesn't move. Dancers usually wear traditional Irish costumes. The music they dance to is played by an Irish folk band. They play instruments like the fiddle and the whistle.

1 **Look at the photos on page 80. Find these things and the action.**

a dress | a traditional costume (x2) | curly hair | to spin | smart trousers

2 **8.07 Read and listen to the article. Which countries do the dances come from?**

3 **Read the article again. Mark the sentences T (true) or F (false).**

0 1st December is the National Tango Day in Argentina. *F*
1 Tango dancers usually wear very nice clothes. ☐
2 Men and women dance the Whirling Dervish. ☐
3 Twenty-four people are involved in a Whirling Dervish performance. ☐
4 The step dance is from Ireland. ☐
5 Step dancers move their whole body. ☐

4 **SPEAKING Are there any special dances in your country? Can you do any of the dances? Discuss with your partner.**

WRITING
Describing a scene

1 **INPUT Read the microblog and look at the photos. Where is Maddie? Tick (✓) the correct photo.**

2 **ANALYSE Read the microblog again. Find examples of the present continuous.**

3 **PLAN Write notes to describe how you are feeling in each of these situations.**

1 You're at a bus stop. It's raining. You're going to meet friends to see a local band play. The bus doesn't come.
2 You're at home. You have to study. The weather outside is very nice and you want to go out, but you have to stay inside.
3 You're at home. You're watching a great film. You want to tell your friends that it's really good.

4 **PRODUCE Use your notes from Exercise 3 to write a microblog for each situation in Exercise 3.**

Remember:

- A microblog message is very short. For example, a Tweet can only be be 280 characters (including spaces).
- Split your microblog into different parts, so you can describe what is happening at different times, and how the situation is changing.

New posts **Profile**

7.22 Here we are. We're waiting. I think there are more than 3,000 people here! It's fantastic. People are singing and smiling – great!

comment Share

7.28 I think they're coming out now. Yes – here they are! Everyone is shouting and cheering!! And the band are smiling. They're very happy.

comment Share

7.49 They're playing my favourite song! I'm so happy and my friends are smiling and singing. I'm watching my favourite band – this is the best!

comment Share

A ☐

B ☐

LISTENING

3-option multiple choice

1 8.08 **You will hear five short conversations. There is one question for each conversation. For each question choose the right answer (A, B or C).**

1 What time does Bob get home from school?

A ☐ B ☐ C ☐

2 When is Sue's birthday?

A ☐ B ☐ C ☐

3 What is Lucy's favourite month?

A ☐ B ☐ C ☐

4 Which instrument does Mike play?

A ☐ B ☐ C ☐

5 Which of Jenny's clothes does Liam like?

A ☐ B ☐ C ☐

READING AND WRITING

Open cloze

2 **Write ONE word in each space to complete the text.**

5G 30%

Joaquim

Hi Sylvie,

I'm sorry, but I [0] ***can't*** come to your place tonight. It's the big match tonight and I want [1] __________ watch it on TV. I know you've [2] __________ a TV, too, but I really want to watch the game with my dad. He's a big football fan, [3] __________ mum isn't, and dad [4] __________ like watching sport on TV alone.

I hope that's OK – please don't be angry with me! Let's go cycling together [5] __________ Sunday – I'll call you.

See you,

Joaquim

TEST YOURSELF UNITS 7 & 8

VOCABULARY

1 Complete the sentences with the words in the list. There are two extra words.

cheering | coat | doing | making | sitting | studying | surf | taking | third | three | trainers | volleyball

1 It's cold outside. Put a ______________________ on when you go out.
2 I love playing ______________________ .
3 We like ______________________ in the park on hot summer days.
4 I'm in the kitchen. I'm ______________________ pizzas for the party.
5 My brother is in Canada. He's ______________________ French at a university there.
6 You can't wear ______________________ to a party! Wear your new shoes.
7 My brother's at the sports centre. He's ______________________ Taekwondo.
8 I love ______________________ photos of different sports.
9 My birthday? It's on the ______________________ of January.
10 They're winning! Everyone is ______________________ !

/10

GRAMMAR

2 Complete the sentences with the words in the list.

can | can't | don't | like | stand | standing

1 Do you ______________________ reading magazines?
2 I don't like ______________________ on the train.
3 I'm ill. I ______________________ go out today.
4 I don't want to sit down. I can ______________________ and watch. It's OK.
5 We really ______________________ like going surfing in winter.
6 He ______________________ run 400 metres in 70 seconds.

3 Find and correct the mistake in each sentence.

1 He can to count to 20 in Spanish.
2 Please be quiet. I'm study for the test next Monday.
3 He doesn't can speak German.
4 I don't like play tennis.
5 She's in town right now. She shops.
6 Does she can play the piano?

/12

FUNCTIONAL LANGUAGE

4 Write the missing words.

don't | how | let's | o'clock | time | to | wearing | what's

1 A ______________________ the time?
B It's four ______________________ . I'm bored!
A Me, too. Why ______________________ we play a game?
B A game? No thanks. ______________________ about going cycling?

2 A Look at those people! They're ______________________ very strange clothes.
B Yes, they're going to a big party in the park. It's a holiday today!
A What ______________________ does the party start?
B At three o'clock. Oh, look! It's quarter ______________________ three now!
______________________ go and join them.

/8

MY SCORE /30

22–30 😊 | 10–21 😐 | 0–9 😣

9 WHO'S HUNGRY?

Get THINKING

Watch the video and think: what is your favourite food?

OBJECTIVES

FUNCTIONS:
talking about food and eating habits; talking about obligation; asking nicely and offering; offering and asking for help

GRAMMAR:
must / mustn't; can (asking for permission); *I'd like ... / Would you like ...?*

VOCABULARY:
food and drink; meals

READING

1 **Match the words in the list with the photos. Write 1–6 in the boxes.**

1 carrot cake | 2 a chef | 3 an omelette
4 some salad | 5 steak | 6 tomato soup

2 SPEAKING **Work in pairs. What other food words do you know?**

pizza, apples, hamburgers, ...

3 SPEAKING **Tell your partner what food you like and don't like.**

I like ... I don't like ...

4 **Look at the photos on page 85. What is unusual about the chefs? Read the article quickly and check your ideas.**

5 9.01 **Read and listen to the article again. Mark the sentences T (true), F (false) or DS (doesn't say).**

0 Harry wants to be star chef. T
1 He is ten years old and he's from New York. ____
2 His sister likes cooking, too, but she's not very good. ____
3 The other children on the TV show aren't very good cooks. ____
4 Children must be ten years old to be on *Kitchen Kids*. ____
5 The chefs' hands must be clean. ____
6 It's OK for the children to eat the food they are cooking. ____
7 After the TV show, Harry goes home to study. ____

KITCHEN KIDS

Harry doesn't want to be a star chef when he's 20. He wants to be one now. This is why he's on the TV programme *Kitchen Kids*.

The ten-year-old New Yorker likes cooking. He can make fantastic soups and salads, excellent omelettes and the best cakes. But there are many other children on the show, too. And they are all very good.

More and more young people are interested in cooking. Many of them learn it from their parents. Others watch special cooking videos for children on YouTube©. In many cities, there are special cooking classes for young people. Some of them are for children from the age of three!

But what must you do to become a star chef? Of course, it's important that you like cooking and are really good at it. But there are some rules. You must be nine years old or more to be on *Kitchen Kids*.

'We must wash our hands before we start cooking,' Harry says. 'And of course we mustn't put them in our mouths. A chef doesn't do that! And we must be very careful with hot plates.'

The show starts. Harry is excited. He knows he's an excellent cook. This time he makes tomato soup, some salad, steak and carrot cake. The experts in the studio love Harry's food, and he stays on the show.

It's 5 pm. The show is over. Harry is happy, and a little tired. He goes home. It's time to do his homework.

TH!NK values

How you eat is important

6 SPEAKING **How often do you do these things? Write *always*, *sometimes*, *often* or *never*. Then tell the class.**

- ☐ a sit at a table to eat ______
- ☐ b eat alone ______
- ☐ c eat slowly ______
- ☐ d eat very fast ______
- ☐ e eat with other people ______
- ☐ f eat and play computer games at the same time ______

I always eat slowly. I sometimes eat with other people.

7 **Look again at the things in Exercise 6. Are they good things to do? Write 1–3 in the boxes: 1 = a good thing to do, 2 = an OK thing to do, 3 = a bad thing to do.**

8 SPEAKING **Work in pairs and compare your ideas.**

I often eat …

I think … is good.

I think … is not so good.

GRAMMAR
must / mustn't

1 Look at the article on page 85. Complete the sentences with *must* or *mustn't*. Then complete the rule.

1 You ____________ be nine years old or more to be on *Kitchen Kids*.
2 We ____________ wash our hands before we start cooking.
3 We ____________ put them in our mouths.

> **RULE:** We use *must* and *mustn't* to talk about rules.
> Use [4]____________ to say that it's necessary to do something.
> Use [5]____________ to say that it's not OK to do something.

Meat

0 *chicken* 1 ________ 2 ________ 3 ________

Fruit

4 ________ 5 ________ 6 ________ 7 ________

Vegetables

8 ________ 9 ________ 10 ________ 11 ________

Drinks

12 ________ 13 ________ 14 ________ 15 ________

2 Complete the dialogues. Use *must* or *mustn't* and a verb from the list.

buy | eat | forget | go

0 A Jasper's got a new cat.
B Oh, really. We *must go* and see it.
1 A Mum, can I have some ice cream?
B Of course not! You know you ______________ ice cream before lunch.
2 A Hey, can I read that book?
B Sure, but you ______________ to give it back. It's my brother's.
3 A Oh, no. There isn't any cheese.
B I ______________ some for the spaghetti bolognese.

3 SPEAKING **Work in pairs. Think of some things that are important for you to do (or not do) in the next few days.**

I must ring my grandma.

I mustn't forget to finish my History project.

→ workbook page 82

VOCABULARY
Food and drink

4 9.02 **Write the names of the food and drinks under the photos. Listen and check.**

5 SPEAKING **Work in pairs. Say which word in each group is different. Why?**

0 coffee – (potato) – tea
1 banana – orange – hamburger
2 carrot – chicken – beef
3 milk – strawberry – apple
4 pepper – potato – orange juice

Number 0 is potato – coffee and tea are drinks.

6 SPEAKING **Look again at the food words in Exercise 4. Work in pairs. Ask and answer questions to find three things you both like.**

Do you like strawberries?

Yes, I love them. And you?

I like them. Do you like ...?

→ workbook page 84

LISTENING

7 **Look at the photo. What can you see?**

8 9.03 **Listen to the dialogue. What do they decide to eat in the end?**

9 9.03 **Listen again. Put the sentences in the order you hear them. Write 1–6 in the boxes.**

- [ ] a Can we do that later?
- [1] b Can we make some sandwiches, Dad?
- [ ] c Can we use this cheese, Dad?
- [ ] d There are some tomatoes.
- [ ] e Would you like some help?
- [ ] f Can we go for fish and chips, Dad?

GRAMMAR

can (asking for permission)

10 **Match these answers to the questions in Exercise 9. Then read the rule.**

1 Mmm … OK. Yes, we can. [ ]
2 No, we can't. [ ]
3 No. Your mum wants that for the lasagne. [ ]

> **RULE:** We use *can* + subject to ask if it's OK to do something.

11 9.04 **Complete the questions with *can* and a verb from the list. Listen and check.**

| ~~do~~ | eat | go out | play | try on | use |

0 *Can* I *do* my homework later?
1 ________ I ________ these jeans, please?
2 ________ I ________ your laptop, please?
3 Dad, ________ I ________ tonight?
4 ________ we ________ football in the garden?
5 ________ we ________ dinner in front of the TV?

12 **Match the answers with the questions in Exercise 11.**

- [0] a No, you can't. Do it now.
- [ ] b Of course you can. But be careful.
- [ ] c No, you can't. You've got school tomorrow.
- [ ] d Sorry, I need it to write some emails.
- [ ] e Yes, the changing room is over there.
- [ ] f Well, OK … , it's your birthday.

→ workbook page 82

SPEAKING

13 **Think about what is true for you. Choose 1–5 (1 = certainly true, 5 = certainly not true).**

1 I often eat between meals. 1 – 2 – 3 – 4 – 5
2 I always eat breakfast. 1 – 2 – 3 – 4 – 5
3 I eat fruit and vegetables every day. 1 – 2 – 3 – 4 – 5
4 I drink lots of water. 1 – 2 – 3 – 4 – 5
5 I eat lots of sweets. 1 – 2 – 3 – 4 – 5
6 I brush my teeth after every meal. 1 – 2 – 3 – 4 – 5

14 **Work in pairs. Compare your answers with a partner.**

I often eat between meals.

I eat fruit every day.

15 **Discuss your answers with the rest of the class. Does everyone have the same answers?**

READING

1 **Read the menu. What food on it would you like?**

2 9.05 **Read and listen to the dialogue. What does Emma eat? What does Oscar eat?**

Server Hello. Can I help you?
Emma Hi. Yes, we'd like a table for two, please.
Server Here are the menus.
Oscar Thanks.
Server What would you like to drink?
Emma I'd like an orange juice.
Oscar And I'd like water, please.
Server Great.
(Two minutes later)
Server Are you ready to order now?
Emma Yes, I'd like the pizza with salad.
Server Any starters?
Emma No, thanks.
Server Would you like any extra toppings on the pizza? Onion, peppers or tomatoes?
Emma Some peppers, please.
Server And what would you like?
Oscar I'd like the chicken and chips.
Server OK. Is that everything?
Oscar Yes, thank you.
(Half an hour later ...)
Server Would you like a dessert?
Oscar Yes, please. I'd like the fruit salad with vanilla ice cream.
Emma Me, too.
(Ten minutes later ...)
Server How are your desserts?
Oscar Great.
Server Would you like any more drinks?
Emma No, thanks. We'd like the bill, please.
Server Of course.

Apple Tree CAFÉ

MENU

OUR STARTERS

Watermelon and cheese salad **£5.25**
Salad (tuna fish and tomato) **£7.50**
Tomato soup **£6.60**

OUR MAIN COURSES

Four-cheese pizza **£9.50**
(extra toppings – onion, peppers, tomatoes)
Pasta with tomato sauce **£8.50**
Fish and chips **£8.50**
Chicken and chips **£7.80**
Cheese and tomato sandwich **£6.50**
Jacket potato **£5.20**

OUR DESSERTS

Fruit salad **£2.40**
banana, strawberry, mango, apple and grapes
Ice cream (per scoop) **£1.20**
Vanilla, strawberry, lemon and chocolate
Chocolate pudding **£1.20**

OUR DRINKS

Fruit juice (orange or apple) **£1.90**
Coffee **£2.20**
Tea **£1.60**
Hot chocolate **£2.10**
Water **£1.10**

3 **Who says these things in a restaurant? Write S (server) or C (customer) in the boxes.**

0 Can I help you? S
1 A table for two, please. ☐
2 Here are the menus. ☐
3 Are you ready to order? ☐
4 I'd like the vegetable soup. ☐
5 What would you like to drink? ☐
6 Can we have the bill, please? ☐
7 Would you like a dessert? ☐

4 SPEAKING **Work in pairs. Look again at the menu and think of more food to add.**

GRAMMAR

I'd like ... / Would you like ...?

5 Complete these sentences from the dialogue on page 88. Then complete the rule.

1 And what ___________ you like?
2 ___________ like the chicken and chips.
3 Would you ___________ a dessert?
4 ___________ like the bill, please.

> **RULE:** We use *I* + *would* (*'d*) + [5]___________ to ask for something in a nice way.
> We use *Would* + *you* + [6]___________ ... ? to offer something.

6 How do you say *Would you like ...?* and *I'd like ...* in your language?

7 Put the words in the correct order to make sentences or questions.

0 like / a / I'd / please / banana .
I'd like a banana, please.
1 like / some / you / Would / coffee ?
____
2 like / fish / I'd / and / , please / chips .
____
3 you / What / to / would / like / eat ?
____
4 to / We'd / like / here / sit .
____
5 would / this afternoon / What / you / to / like / do ?
____

8 Complete these sentences.

1 ___________ to order now?
2 ___________ some coffee?
3 We ___________ to sit there, please.
4 I ___________ some ice cream, please.

9 SPEAKING Work in groups. One of you is the server at the Apple Tree Café, the others order food and drinks. Act out the situation. Then switch roles.

→ workbook page 83

PRONUNCIATION
Intonation – giving two choices Go to page 121.

VOCABULARY

Meals

10 9.08 Match the words in the list to the items in the picture. Write 1–9 in the boxes. Listen and check.

1 bread | **2** butter | **3** cereal | **4** egg | **5** fruit
6 honey | **7** jam | **8** toast | **9** yoghurt

11 SPEAKING Copy the table into your notebook and complete it. Then tell the class.

	always	often	sometimes	never
breakfast				
lunch				
dinner				

For breakfast, I always drink ...

I never have (any) ... for lunch.

→ workbook page 84

WRITING

A meal plan for your friend

12 Ask a partner to give you his/her table from Exercise 11. Imagine he/she is staying at your house for two days. You want to make meals that he/she likes. Write a menu for your partner for both days.

SATURDAY		SUNDAY	
	Breakfast:		Breakfast:
	Lunch:		Lunch:
	Dinner:		Dinner:

13 SPEAKING Show your ideas to your partner. Is he/she happy with the meals?

DEVELOPING SPEAKING

1 **Look at the photo. What is Jo doing?**

2 9.09 **Now read and listen to the dialogue. What happens to Jo's lasagne?**

Mum: Wow! What a great smell!

Jo: Thanks, Mum. It's lasagne. It's in the oven and it's almost ready.

Mum: Lasagne from the shop?

Jo: No, Mum, it's my lasagne. It's got meat, pepper, mushrooms, cheese, onion – everything. And we can eat it with a bit of salad.

Mum: Oh, right. But, we? Who's coming for lunch?

Jo: Mark and Chloe. We want to study together this afternoon, and have lunch together first. That's OK, right?

Mum: Of course, Jo. But …

Jo: But what, Mum?

Mum: Well, the thing is, I'd like a nice, quiet afternoon.

Jo: Oh, don't worry, Mum. After lunch, we plan to study upstairs in my room.

Jo: Ah! It's ready.

Mum: Be careful, Jo. It's very hot. Can I help you?

Jo: It's OK, Mum. I can just … Oh, no! My lasagne! It's all over the floor. Now what?

Mum: Well, first, let's clean it all up. And then … do you and your friends want to go to the new sandwich shop?

Jo: Not really. But I've got an idea, Mum. We can just have the salad!

Mum: OK. And you and I can make some chocolate-covered bananas, so your friends can have some dessert, too.

Jo: Thanks, Mum, you're the best!

3 SPEAKING **Read the dialogue again. Answer the questions with a partner.**

1 Who cooked the lasagne?
2 Who is coming to have lunch with Jo?
3 What does Jo's mum want this afternoon?
4 What can Jo do to fix the problem?

Phrases for fluency

4 **Find the expressions 1–4 in the dialogue. Who says them? How do you say them in your language?**

1 Of course. ____________
2 Be careful … ____________
3 a bit (of) … ____________
4 the thing is, … ____________

5 **Put the sentences in the correct order to make a dialogue.**

☐ **Harry** Well, the thing is, I want to cook some Indian food.
☑ 1 **Harry** Do you like Indian food?
☐ **Harry** Yes, but I don't know how to cook.
☐ **Claire** Oh. And you need a bit of help.
☐ **Claire** Of course. I love curry and stuff. Why?
☐ **Claire** OK. You can use my mum's cookbook. But be careful! She loves that book!

6 **Complete the dialogues with the expressions from Exercise 4.**

1 A Let's go to the cinema tonight.
B No thanks. I've got [1]____________ work to do.
A Really? On Saturday?
B No, not really. I'm sorry. [2]____________, I haven't got any money.

2 A Can I look at your new phone?
B [3]____________. Here it is.
A Oh, it's really nice!
B Thanks, I love it. Oh, [4]____________! Don't break it!

FUNCTIONS
Offering and asking for help

KEY LANGUAGE

Can you …?	Do you want …?
Can I …?	Thank you. / No, thank you.

7 **Complete the dialogues using the phrases from the Key Language box.**

A [1]____________ help me for a moment?
B Of course. What would you like me to do?
A [2]____________. I need some help cleaning the kitchen.
A [3]____________ help you with anything?
B [4]____________. I'm OK.

8 **Work in pairs. Think of a situation where you would ask for or offer help. Write a dialogue. Use phrases from the Key Language box.**

9 SPEAKING **Act out your dialogues from Exercise 8.**

LIFE COMPETENCIES

We all want to do the things that we want to do – it makes us feel good. But thinking about other people, helping them and making them happy, can make us feel good, too.

1 ▶27 **Watch the vlog. Why can't Becky eat the pizza?**

2 ▶27 **Watch the vlog again. Match the food to the people in Becky's family.**

A

____

B

____

C

____

3 **Read the dialogues. Who do you think says these things?**

1 What a lovely party.
2 Thanks for dinner, guys.

Mike I'm hungry. Let's phone and get some Indian food.
Emma Curry! Yes! That's a great idea.
Mike Oh, just a minute. The thing is, Peter doesn't like Indian food very much.
Emma Oh, don't worry, he'll be OK with a curry.
Mike No, I don't think so. Let's get pizza. He likes pizza.
Emma Well, yes, OK. Pizza's good, too. Where's the phone?

Olivia What are you doing?
Laura I'm choosing the music for the family party.
Olivia Cool. Is *What a Wonderful World* on the list?
Laura Of course not! It's old!
Olivia But Grandma and Grandad are coming to the party, and it's their favourite song.
Laura Oh, yes. You're right. OK, where can I find it?

4 SPEAKING **Ask and answer the questions with a partner.**

1 Who is thinking about other people?
2 What do they decide to do?

Me and my world

5 SPEAKING **How can you show these people you are thinking about them?**

1 Your dad is travelling a lot for work.
2 Your brother is studying hard for some important exams.
3 Your best friend has a broken leg and is in bed for three weeks.

6 SPEAKING **How does it feel when someone thinks about you? Tell your partner.**

TIPS FOR THINKING ABOUT OTHER PEOPLE

- Think about how your actions can change other people's feelings.
- Remember to ask how other people feel.
- Ask yourself: 'Does this person need help?' or 'Is what I am doing OK for them, too?'

10 BIG SUCCESSES

Get THINKING

Watch the video and think:
When do you feel proud of yourself?

OBJECTIVES

FUNCTIONS: talking about achievements; talking about the past; asking for information about the past; talking about the weather

GRAMMAR: past simple: *was / wasn't, were / weren't, there was / were*; past simple: *Was he …? / Were you …?*; past simple: regular verbs

VOCABULARY: time expressions: past; the weather

READING

1 **Match the words in the list with the photos. Write 1–6 in the boxes.**

1 astronaut | **2** competition | **3** factory
4 skydiving | **5** spacecraft | **6** stamps

2 SPEAKING **Look at the photos and answer the questions.**

1 What are the names of the two people?
2 Where were they from?
3 Why are they famous?

3 SPEAKING **Name some famous people in your country. Why are they famous?**

… is really famous in our country.

That's true! It's because …

4 10.01 **Read and listen to the article and answer the question.**

Why is Valentina Tereshkova famous?

5 **Read the article again and put the events in order.**

a She was named 'Woman of the Century'. ☐
b Tereshkova was in space for three days. ☐
c She was the carrier of the Olympic flag. ☐
d There was a competition to find new astronauts. ☐
e Valentina Tereshkova was born. ☐
f She was on a training programme. ☐

SHE WAS THE FIRST WOMAN IN SPACE

Posted 26th May

Valentina Tereshkova was born in Russia on 6th March 1937. Her father was a driver and her mother was a factory worker. Valentina was a worker in a factory, too. Her hobby was skydiving and it was her dream to be an astronaut and to go into space.

In 1962, there was a big competition to find new astronauts. There were 400 people interested in going to space. The training programme wasn't very easy, but Tereshkova was hard-working. And she was the lucky one. Tereshkova's big day was 16th June 1963, and she was ready.

The name of her spacecraft was Vostok 6, and Tereshkova was the first woman in space. The flight was very difficult because there were many technical problems and Tereshkova wasn't very well for most of the flight. She was in space for three days. She is the only woman to fly into space alone. After that, she was very famous all over the world. Her face was on stamps in many countries.

In the year 2000, there was a big celebration in London, and Valentina Tereshkova was named the 'Woman of the Century'.

At the opening ceremony of the Winter Olympics in Russia in 2014, Valentina Tereshkova was one of the carriers of the Olympic flag.

These were very important moments for her.

TH!NK values

Hard work and achievement

6 **In 2000, Valentina Tereshkova was named 'Woman of the Century'. Which of the following, do you think, were important for her success? Write N (not important) or I (important).**

1 She was born in 1937. ☐
2 Her mother was a factory worker. ☐
3 Her hobby was skydiving. ☐
4 It was her dream to be an astronaut and go into space. ☐
5 She was hard-working in the training programme. ☐
6 The name of her spacecraft was Vostok 6. ☐
7 The flight was difficult, but Tereshkova was strong. ☐
8 She was in space for three days. ☐

7 SPEAKING **Work in pairs and compare your answers. Do you agree?**

She was born in 1937. I think that was important for her success because it was the start of space travel.

I agree. / I don't agree. I think …

GRAMMAR
Past simple: *was / wasn't; were / weren't; there was / were*

1 Complete the sentences from the article on page 93. Then complete the rule and the table.

1 Valentina Tereshkova ___________ born on 6th March 1937.
2 The training programme ___________ very easy.
3 There ___________ 400 people interested in going to space.
4 These ___________ very important moments for her.

RULE: *was/were* is the past form of [5]___________ .

Positive	Negative
I/he/she/it [6]___________ . We/you/they were. There was / [7]___________ .	I/he/she/it wasn't (was not). We/you/they [8]___________ (were not). There [9]___________ / weren't.

2 Complete the sentences with *was, wasn't, were* or *weren't*.

1 My friends and I [0] *were* in the park last Sunday. My brother [1]___________ there, too, but my parents [2]___________ there because they [3]___________ at the cinema.
2 There [4]___________ lots of people in the park. There [5]___________ a boy with his grandparents. They [6]___________ nice people. The boy's name [7]___________ Ollie.

→ workbook page 90

VOCABULARY
Time expressions: past

3 🔊 10.02 Write *at, in, last* and *yesterday* to complete the time expressions. Listen and check.

1 ___________ weekend / Sunday / night / week / month / year
2 ___________ morning / afternoon / evening
3 ___________ 2014
4 ___________ four o'clock / 5.30 / 6 am / 6 pm

4 Look at the pictures. Write sentences to say where the people were and when. Use *at, in, last* or *yesterday*.

at the bookshop | in Rome | in the park | at a birthday party
at the shopping centre | at his friends' house

Eliza was at the shopping centre at ten yesterday morning.

5 Make notes about where you were yesterday at the times in the pictures A–D in Exercise 4.

6 SPEAKING Work in pairs. Tell your partner where you were yesterday.

I was in town at ten yesterday morning. What about you?

I was at home.

7 SPEAKING Use the information about your partner to report to the class.

Yesterday morning, Maria was at home. At half past three yesterday afternoon, she was at a friend's house. In the evening, she was at her grandma's house.

→ workbook page 92

LISTENING

8 **Look at the picture. Where was Alice yesterday? Why wasn't Will there?**

9 🔊 10.03 **Listen to the dialogue and check your ideas.**

10 🔊 10.03 **Listen again. Match the questions with the answers.**

0 Does Alice say the prize-giving was good? [*e*]
1 Were there many parents there? [ ]
2 Was Tom Hammond the best student of the year? [ ]
3 Who was the best sportsperson of the year? [ ]
4 What was Alice's prize? [ ]
5 How does Will feel about Alice? [ ]

a No, there weren't.
b It was Tom Hammond.
c He's proud of her.
d No, it was his sister, Sandra.
e No, she says it wasn't.
f A book about science.

GRAMMAR
Past simple: *Was he …? / Were you …?*

11 **Put the words in the correct order to make questions.**

1 the teachers / all / Were / there / ?
____
2 she / last year / Was / the best student / ?
____
3 nice / the / Was / prize / something / ?
____

12 **Match the answers below with the questions in Exercise 11. Then complete the table.**

a Yes, it was. [ ]
b No, she wasn't. [ ]
c No, they weren't. [ ]

Question	Short answer
Was I/he/she/it … ?	Yes, I/he/she was.
[1] __________ we/you/they … ?	No, I/he/she [2] __________ .
	Yes, we/you/they [3] __________ .
	No, we/you/they weren't.

13 🔊 10.04 **Complete the dialogue with *was, were, wasn't* or *weren't*. Then listen and check.**

Fiona Oh, no!
Raj What's the matter?
Fiona My phone? Where is it? It [0] *was* in my jacket!
Raj OK, calm down. Where [1] __________ your phone this morning?
Fiona Well, I [2] __________ at home from nine o'clock to ten o'clock.
Raj And then? [3] __________ you in town?
Fiona Yes, I [4] __________ . I [5] __________ in the shopping centre. And I'm 100% sure that my phone [6] __________ in my pocket.
Raj [7] __________ Steve and Maisie with you?
Fiona No, they [8] __________ . I [9] __________ in the shoe shop. I bought some new shoes.
Raj Wait a minute. Let me call you.
Fiona It's ringing! Oh, look! It's in the shoe bag! It [10] __________ there all the time!

→ workbook page 90

FUNCTIONS
Asking for information about the past

14 **Write *was* or *were* to complete the questions. Then ask and answer the questions with a partner. Check your answers on page 93.**

1 __________ Valentina Tereshkova born in Russia?
2 __________ her parents astronauts, too?
3 __________ there 400 people interested in the competition?
4 __________ the flight very easy or very difficult?
5 __________ the Winter Olympics in Russia in 2015?

15 **Make notes to answer the following questions.**

1 Where were you at 3 pm on Saturday?
2 What was your hobby when you were eight?
3 How old were you in May 2019?
4 How old was your best friend last year?

16 SPEAKING **Work in pairs. Ask and answer the questions in Exercise 15.**

READING

1 **Look at the photos of people doing difficult things. Which ones do you think are easy? Hard? Fun?**

I think photo 1 is ... *Maybe photo 2 is ...*

2 10.05 **Read and listen to the chat. Write the correct name beside the photos.**

SPORTS ACHIEVERS

Yesterday, I was online and I learned about a woman called Amy who walked all round the UK to get money for charity. And in winter! When there was rain and snow! Do you know any other amazing stories like that?

A ______

Jenny *(Five minutes ago)*
How about Dee Caffari? She sailed around the world, non-stop, three times! That's right, three times. Imagine the wind and the rain! Fantastic, eh?

B ______

Sam *(20 minutes ago)*
OK, well there's a boy called Jordan Romero, from the US – he climbed Mount Everest when he was 13 years old. It's really cold up there, but he managed to get to the top. Only 13! Now that's an achievement.

C ______

Martha *(25 minutes ago)*
My friend Corey Armstrong decided to run a marathon when he was 16. He finished in just over four hours. He enjoyed it a lot, so then he decided to do the marathon in Death Valley in the US. It's so hot there – often more than 40 degrees Celsius. This time he was slower, almost five hours – but I still think it's fantastic. 42km when it's over 40 degrees! I think he almost died!

D ______

Mark *(32 minutes ago)*
Before 1926, a lot of women tried to swim the cold water of the English Channel from England to France – but they all failed. But in 1926, Gertrude Ederle (an Olympic gold medal swimmer) arrived on an English beach after 14 hours and 31 minutes. She returned to her home in New York a hero! How about that!?

E ______

3 **Read the chat again. Mark the sentences T (true) or F (false).**

0 Dee Caffari sailed around the world alone. *T*
1 She sailed around the world four times. ☐
2 Jordan Romero was 13 when he climbed Mount Everest. ☐
3 Corey Armstrong finished his first marathon in 3 hours 50 minutes. ☐
4 He finished the Death Valley marathon in the same time. ☐
5 Gertrude Ederle was the first woman to try to swim the English Channel. ☐
6 Gertrude's cross-channel swim was from France to England. ☐

4 SPEAKING **Do you know any amazing sports achievers? Tell your partner.**

Train to TH!NK

Sequencing

5 **Put the sentences in order to tell Girl Hero's story.**

☐ There was a very fast car on the road.
8 Everyone was very happy.
☐ There were also two young boys in the road.
1 It was a hot day and Girl Hero wanted an ice cream.
☐ She walked to an ice cream shop.
☐ Girl Hero jumped in front of the car and stopped it with her hand.
☐ She saved the boys.
☐ She walked out of the shop with her ice cream.

6 SPEAKING **Work in pairs. Tell the story. Can you include these lines?**

She walked back home. *Girl Hero started to run.* *The boys smiled.*

GRAMMAR

Past simple: regular verbs

7 Write the base form of the verbs.

Base form	0 *finish*	1 ______	2 ______	3 ______
Past simple	finished	sailed	decided	tried

8 Complete the sentences from the text on page 96 with the past forms from Exercise 7. Then complete the rule.

1 Dee Caffari ____________ around the world three times.
2 My friend Corey ____________ to run a marathon when he was 16.
3 He ____________ in just over four hours.
4 A lot of women ____________ to swim across the English Channel.

> **RULE:** To form the past simple of regular verbs, add [5]____________ to the base form.
> When the verb ends in *-e*, add *-d*.
> When the verb ends in consonant + *-y*, change *y* to [6]____________ and add *-ed*.

9 Write the past simple forms of these verbs. Check your answers in the text on page 96.

1 learn ____________ 4 die ____________
2 walk ____________ 5 try ____________
3 climb ____________ 6 arrive ____________

10 Complete the text about Simone Biles. Use the past simple form of the verbs in brackets.

SIMONE BILES

Simone Biles was born in 1997. When she was six, she [0] *visited* a gym, and she [1]__________ (try) gymnastics for the first time. She [2]__________ (love) it! She [3]__________ (join) the gym and [4]__________ (work) hard to become a great gymnast.
In 2013, at the World Championships, she [5]__________ (invent) a new move, and now the move is called 'the Biles'.
In the 2016 Olympics, she [6]__________ (finish) first in five events and won four gold medals. She also [7]__________ (carry) the US flag at the closing ceremony.

→ workbook page 91

PRONUNCIATION
Past simple regular verbs Go to page 121.

VOCABULARY

The weather

11 10.08 Match the sentences in the list with the pictures. Write 1–8 in the boxes. Listen and check.

1 It's cloudy. | 2 It's cold. | 3 It's hot.
4 It's raining. | 5 It's snowing.
6 It's sunny. | 7 It's warm. | 8 It's windy.

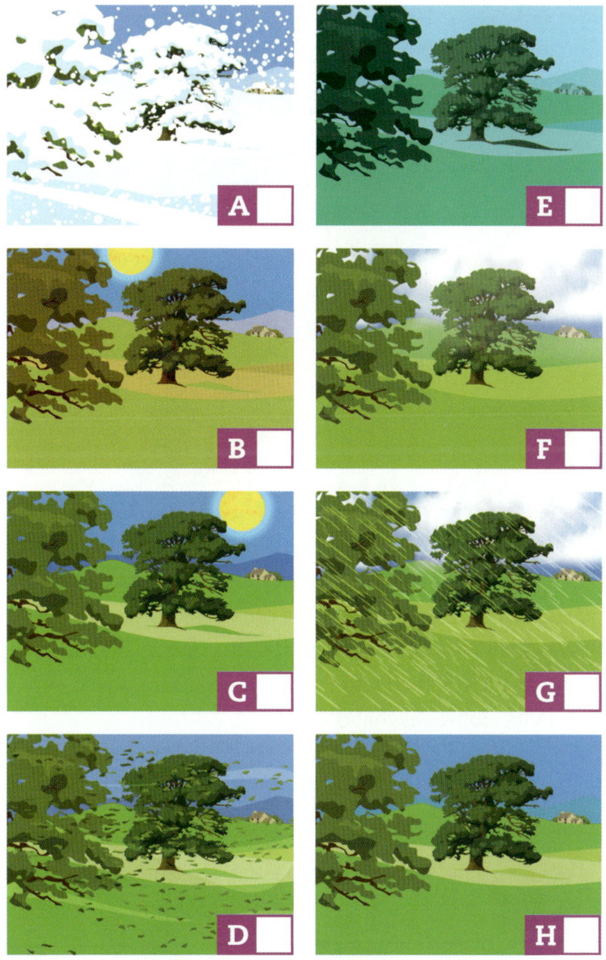

12 Complete the dialogues with some of the phrases from Exercise 11. Sometimes there is more than one correct answer.

0 A What's the weather like?
B *It's raining*. Take an umbrella.
1 A Bye, Mum.
B Bye. But you don't need a jumper. ____________ outside.
2 A Hey look! ____________!
B Great! We can go skiing later!
3 A Wow, ____________ today.
B I know! You must hold on to your hat!

13 SPEAKING Work in pairs. Write similar dialogues and act them out.

→ workbook page 92

TH!NK

Statues around the world

Culture

STATUES

There are many wonderful statues all over the world. Many of them help us to remember the lives of great people.

ROSA PARKS

One day in 1965, a bus driver in Alabama, in the US, asked Rosa Parks to give a man her seat – because he was white, and she was black. She said 'No,' and the police decided to take her away. It was a very important moment in the history of black people's rights in the US. The statue shows Rosa sitting on a rock, wearing the same clothes as that day in 1965.

FRANZ KAFKA

Franz Kafka was a writer from Prague. He was born in 1883. His books were in German. During his life he was not very famous, but now he is. Many of his stories were very strange. There's a very unusual statue of him in Prague. He's sitting on the shoulders of an empty suit!

'OS CANDANGOS'

'The Candangos' were men who travelled from all over Brazil, between 1956 and 1960, to build the new capital city of Brazil, Brasilia. In 1956, 256 men arrived – but before long, there were 30,000, who worked hard to build the city. Brasilia opened in 1960, and this eight-metre-high statue to remember the 'Candangos' is in the 'Three Powers' square. The two figures are holding digging tools.

SUZANNE LENGLEN

At the Roland Garros tennis centre in Paris, there is a court called Suzanne Lenglen. Lenglen was a famous French tennis player, who played from 1914 to 1926. She was the Number One player for many years. In front of the court is this statue: Lenglen is jumping with a racket in her hand, and she is wearing her famous white dress and headband.

1 **Look at the photos on page 98. Find these things.**

headband | rock
shoulders | suit | tools

2 10.09 **Read and listen to the article. In which city are the statues of Franz Kafka and Suzanne Lenglen?**

3 **Read the article again. Mark the sentences T (true) or F (false).**

0 Rosa Parks was a black American woman. *T*
1 The police took away the man who wanted Rosa's seat. ☐
2 Franz Kafka was from Berlin. ☐
3 Kafka's stories were unusual. ☐
4 The Candangos were from Brasilia. ☐
5 The Candangos statue is life-size. ☐
6 'Suzanne Lenglen' is the name of a tennis centre. ☐
7 Lenglen was famous for tennis and for her clothes. ☐

4 SPEAKING **Do you know any of the people? Do you know any other famous statues? Talk to your partner.**

WRITING
A statue in my town

1 INPUT **Read what Maggie, from Manchester, wrote. Who does she want a statue of, and why?**

2 ANALYSE **Read the text again. Find and underline examples of *was/were* and other verbs in the past simple.**

3 **Which parts of the text talk about these things? Write 1, 2 or 3 in the boxes.**

1 why the person/people should have a statue
2 where the writer is from and who the statue is of
3 what the person/people did

4 PLAN **Imagine you can choose to have a statue of a famous person (or famous people) in your town/city. Make notes about these things:**

1 where you live
2 who the person/people is/are
3 what the person/people did
4 why you think they should have a statue

5 PRODUCE **Use your notes from Exercise 3 to write a short text with the title 'A Statue in My Town'.**

1 Use Maggie's text to help you.
2 Write about 80 words.
3 Check that you used the past simple correctly.

I live in Manchester in England and I think it's a good idea to have a statue here of a band called The Stone Roses. ☐
The band started in 1983 and they only recorded two albums. The first album, in 1989, was a big success. Some people called it 'the best British album of all time'. They were also famous for their clothes, especially the hat one of the band members liked to wear. The band stopped in 1995, but they played more concerts in 2011 and 2012. They also recorded some new songs in 2015. Then, in 2017, they played their final concerts. ☐
I think they were important for Manchester because their music helped people all over the world know about the city. ☐

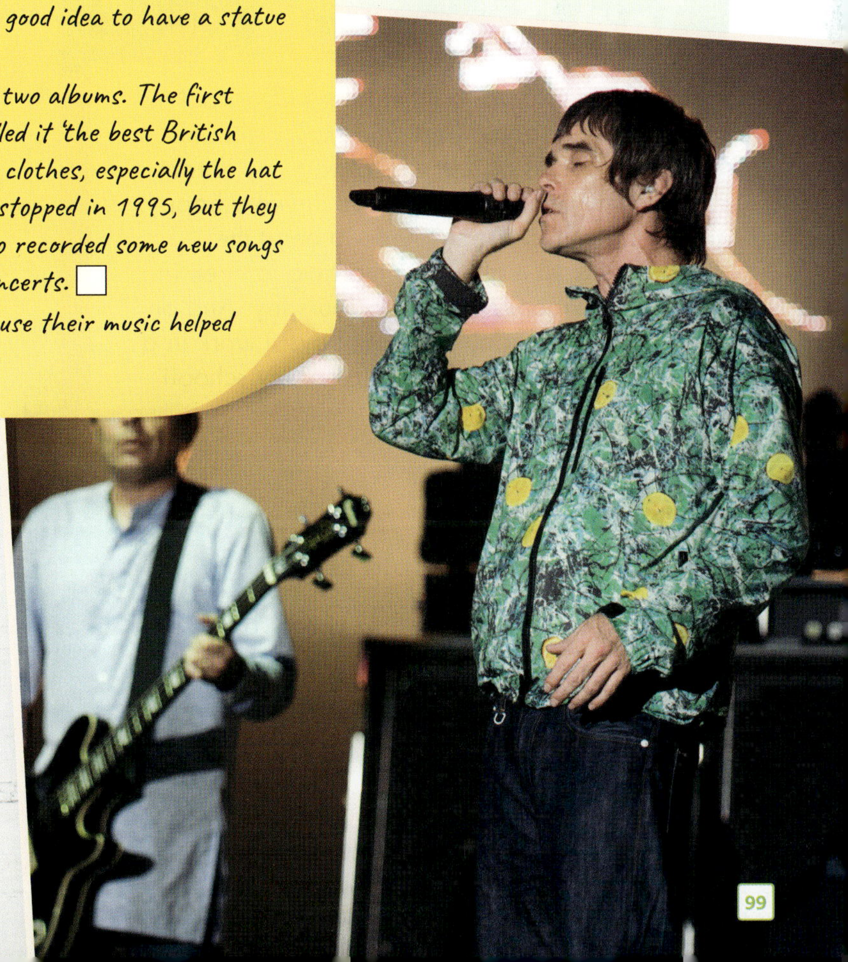

TOWARDS A2 Key for Schools

READING AND WRITING
Multiple matching

1 For these questions, choose the correct answer.

Which person:	James	Maria
1 moved from one country to another?	A	B
2 arrived in London first?	A	B
3 works three days a week?	A	B
4 works and studies?	A	B
5 does not say anything about money?	A	B
6 does not say anything about their dreams for the future?	A	B

James

I'm from Oxford, but I'm at drama school in London. I arrived here and started school three months ago. It was always my dream to study at drama school, so I'm very happy. It's hard because we need to be at the school from eight in the morning to three in the afternoon, Monday to Thursday. And on Fridays, Saturdays and Sundays, I work in a shop to make money to pay for my school!

Maria

I remember arriving in London a year ago, from Spain. It was so exciting. I love it here. I am working for a small IT company. I work six days a week – it's a lot, but for me it's OK. In the future, I want to start my own IT company, and I think this will help me. The people in the company are fun and I'm learning a lot!

LISTENING
3-option multiple choice

2 10.10 **For each question, choose the correct answer.**

1 The new boy is from
- A Mexico.
- B Spain.
- C France.

2 The girl buys
- A shoes.
- B trousers.
- C a coat.

3 The daughter has got
- A a headache.
- B a sore throat.
- C a stomach ache.

4 The son scored
- A no goals.
- B 3 goals.
- C 5 goals.

VOCABULARY

1 Complete the sentences with the words in the list. There are two extra words.

at | carrots | cloudy | in | juice | last | meat | oranges | raining | sandwich | warm | yesterday

1 It's a nice day today. It's ______________________ and sunny.
2 Where were you ______________________ morning?
3 I love vegetables; ______________________ are my favourite.
4 He was born ______________________ 2003.
5 They arrived ______________________ half past five.
6 Would you like a chicken and tomato ______________________ ?
7 It's very ______________________ today. Perhaps there'll be rain later.
8 There was a lot of rain ______________________ night.
9 Do you want something to drink? Some ______________________ , perhaps?
10 No chicken or lamb, thank you. I don't eat ______________________ .

/10

GRAMMAR

2 Complete the sentences with the words in the list.

can | must | mustn't | was | were | would

1 ______________________ you like eggs for breakfast?
2 It ______________________ a very windy day yesterday.
3 It's her birthday tomorrow. We ______________________ remember to say 'Happy Birthday'.
4 ______________________ we watch TV now, please?
5 Meet me at six o'clock, OK? You ______________________ be late!
6 There ______________________ 200 people at the game on Saturday.

3 Find and correct the mistake in each sentence.

1 Last Sunday morning, we play computer games at home.
2 There was five bananas here yesterday. Where are they?
3 I must to study tonight.
4 Can I having a cheese sandwich, please?
5 I tryed to phone you yesterday, but there was no answer.
6 I'm thirsty. I like some water, please.

/12

FUNCTIONAL LANGUAGE

4 Complete the missing words.

1 A Do you want some h _ _ _ with your homework?
B No, t _ _ _ _ _ , I'm OK.
2 A Where were you y _ _ _ _ _ _ _ _ afternoon?
B I w _ _ at home. Why?
3 A Can you o _ _ _ the window, please?
B Yes, of c _ _ _ _ _ .
4 B C _ _ I use your phone, please?
B Sure, no p _ _ _ _ _ _ .

/8

MY SCORE /30

22–30 | 10–21 | 0–9

11 THE ANIMAL WORLD

Get THINKING

Watch the video and think: what are your favourite animals?

OBJECTIVES

FUNCTIONS: asking and answering about past holidays; talking about ability in the past; describing a picture; sequencing (in a story)

GRAMMAR: past simple: irregular verbs; past simple (negative and questions); *could* / *couldn't*

VOCABULARY: verb and noun pairs; adjectives

READING

1 **Match the words in the list with the photos. Write 1–12 in the boxes.**

1 bear | 2 bird | 3 cat | 4 dog | 5 dolphin
6 elephant | 7 gorilla | 8 horse | 9 tiger
10 rabbit | 11 sheep | 12 snake

2 SPEAKING **Complete the sentences with (plural) animals. Use the animals from Exercise 1 or any others that you know. Then compare your ideas with your partner.**

0 Sometimes *snakes* are dangerous.
1 Sometimes you see ______ in people's houses.
2 You can find ______ in towns.
3 You can find ______ in the countryside.
4 I like ______ .
5 I don't like ______ .
6 You can find ______ on a farm.
7 ______ can sometimes run very fast.
8 You find ______ in the sea.
9 People sometimes eat ______ .

3 11.01 **Look at the photos on page 103. What do you think the article is about? Read and listen to the article and check your ideas.**

4 **Read the article again. Choose the correct words.**

0 Davide Ceci was with his *mother* / *father*.
1 Davide was *excited* / *scared* in the water.
2 The dolphin found Davide *on top of* / *under* the water.
3 Davide's *brother* / *father* helped him onto the boat.
4 Adam Walker was in the water in *New Zealand* / *Australia*.
5 Adam saw a *whale* / *shark* in the water.
6 A group of *ten* / *twelve* dolphins swam next to Adam.
7 The dolphins stayed with Adam for *60* / *90* minutes.

DOLPHINS TO THE RESCUE

Everyone knows that dolphins are very intelligent animals. But did you know that many scientists believe there is a special connection between dolphins and humans? There are lots of stories about dolphins helping humans who are in danger. Here are two of our favourites.

14-year-old Davide Ceci was in his father's boat off the south-east coast of Italy when he had an accident and fell into the water. Davide didn't know how to swim and his father didn't see him fall, so he didn't stop the boat. He shouted, but his dad didn't hear him. Davide got very worried. Then, very quickly, a dolphin came to help him. It gave Davide a push back up to the top of the water and the boy got onto the dolphin's back. The dolphin took him back to the boat. When Davide's father saw his son, he pulled him from the water. The dolphin saved Davide's life!

In 2016, Adam Walker went to New Zealand to swim across the Cook Strait between the North and South Islands. He was swimming when he saw a large dark shape below him. He knew that it was a great white shark and his life was in danger. Adam knew he didn't have a lot of time. A few seconds later, a group of ten dolphins joined him and swam in a circle between him and the shark. The circle of dolphins kept Adam safe. After half an hour, the shark left, but the dolphins swam with him for another hour.

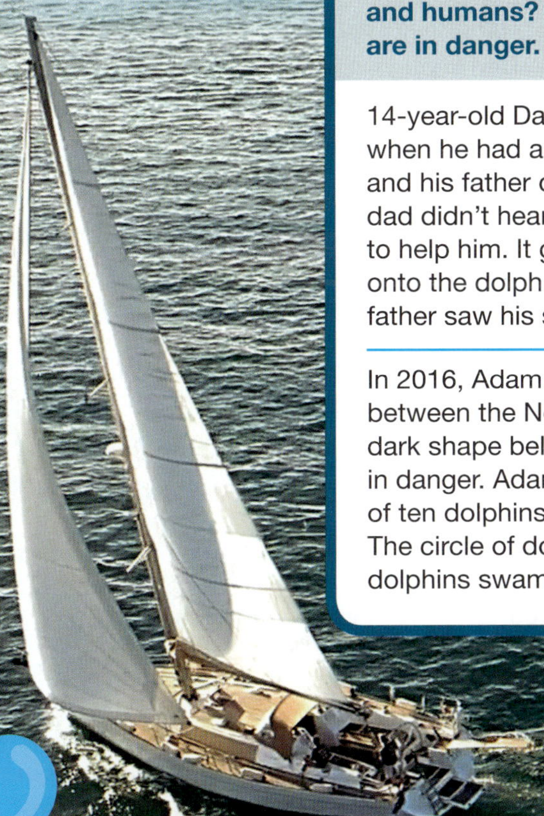

THINK *values*

Animals and us

5 SPEAKING **Dolphins saved the lives of Davide and Adam. Work in pairs. Make a list of things they can do to thank the dolphins.**

6 **Tick (✓) the things you agree with.**

- ☐ It's important to be nice to animals.
- ☐ Animals and people can live together.
- ☐ It isn't good to eat animals.
- ☐ It isn't good to use animals for clothes.
- ☐ All animals are important.
- ☐ Zoos are bad for animals.
- ☐ Zoos help people understand animals.
- ☐ It isn't good to have animals in your house.

7 SPEAKING **Work in pairs and compare your ideas from Exercise 6.**

GRAMMAR

Past simple: irregular verbs

1 Look at these examples from the article on page 103. Find the past tense of the other verbs in article and write them in the table.

The dolphins **swam** with him for another hour.
After half an hour, the shark **left**.

1	swim	*swam*	7	give	
2	leave	*left*	8	go	
3	come		9	know	
4	fall		10	pull	
5	have		11	see	
6	get		12	take	

2 Complete the sentences with the past simple form of the words in the list. Use the irregular verbs list on page 128 of the Workbook to help you.

~~come~~ | drink | eat | fall | forget | get
give | ~~go~~ | run | see | take | write

0 Last weekend we *went* to Ireland. My grandfather *came* with us.
1 We ___________ some interesting places and ___________ lots of photographs.
2 The boy ___________ too fast and he ___________ over.
3 I ___________ some good presents for my birthday. My parents ___________ me a tablet!
4 I ___________ an email to my teacher, but I ___________ to send it!
5 My friends and I went to a fast food place last night. We ___________ hotdogs and we ___________ orange juice.

Past simple (negative)

3 These sentences are not true. Use the article on page 103 to correct them. Then choose the correct words to complete the rule.

0 Davide knew how to swim.
Davide didn't know how to swim.
1 His father saw him fall.
____
2 He stopped the boat.
____

RULE: To make negative sentences in the past simple, we use *didn't* (*did not*) + the [3]*base* / *past* form of the verb.
It's [4]*the same* / *different* for both regular and irregular verbs.
It's [5]*the same* / *different* for all subjects (I/you/they/we/he/she/it).

4 Make these sentences negative.

0 I liked the film. *I didn't like the film.*
1 I saw my friend at the party. ___________
2 We had a good time. ___________
3 I took a photograph. ___________
4 Our friends came to see us. ___________
5 She found her phone. ___________

→ workbook page 100

VOCABULARY

Verb and noun pairs

5 Choose the correct words in the sentences from the article on page 103.

1 Davide *had* / *did* an accident.
2 Davide *got* / *did* very worried.
3 Adam knew he should *do* / *make* something.

6 Write the phrases in the correct columns. Some of the phrases can go in more than one column.

~~a break~~ | a good time | a mistake
a noise | a shower | angry | away
excited | homework | on holiday
photos | something

have	take	make
	a break	

do	get	go

7 To which column(s) can you add the words in this list? Can you add more words to the columns?

a bath | breakfast | fun | a party | skiing | a train

8 Complete the sentences so they are true for you. Use a positive or negative verb form.

1 I ___________ breakfast this morning.
2 I ___________ my homework last night.
3 Last weekend, I ___________ a lot of photos with my phone.
4 I ___________ a good time at the weekend.
5 My family ___________ on holiday last year.
6 The last time I went to a party, I ___________ fun.

9 SPEAKING Work in pairs. Compare your answers with a partner.

→ workbook page 102

LISTENING

10 🔊 11.02 **It's the end of the summer holidays. Mandy meets Josh and asks about his holiday. Listen to their conversation. Tick (✓) the animals Josh saw and cross (✗) the ones he didn't see.**

11 🔊 11.02 **Listen again. Complete the sentences with one word.**

1 Josh's family went to the Pantanal in ____________ for their holidays.
2 Josh's ____________ really likes birds.
3 One night they heard a jaguar outside their ____________ .
4 It was ____________ when Josh heard the jaguar.
5 Most nights they slept in ____________ .
6 Their guide Sergio spoke ____________ .

SPEAKING

12 Tick (✓) the statements that are true for you.

☐ I like camping.
☐ It's exciting to be near animals and nature.
☐ I only want to see animals in a zoo.
☐ I don't like dangerous animals or places.

13 Work in pairs. Talk about the statements in Exercise 12. Do you agree or disagree?

I don't like camping.
Me neither.
I like camping.
Me too.

GRAMMAR
Past simple (questions)

14 Complete the questions from the listening. Write the same word in each space. Then complete the rule.

1 ____________ you have a good holiday?
2 ____________ he speak English?
3 Where ____________ you go?
4 How ____________ you travel around?

RULE: To form past simple questions, we use [5] ____________ + I/you/he/she/it/we/they + the base form of the verb.

15 Put the words in order to make questions.

0 to the party / Did / go / you ?
Did you go to the party?
1 she / a good time / Did / have ?
____
2 watch / on TV / Did / that programme / you ?
____
3 they / a lot of / take / photos / Did ?
____
4 What / for breakfast / did / have / you ?
____
5 did / you / Where / last night / go ?
____

16 Complete the dialogues.

0 **A** What *did you watch* last night?
B I watched a really good film.
1 **A** Where ____________ on Saturday?
B I went to the cinema.
2 **A** What ____________ at the zoo?
B We saw some really cool animals!
3 **A** What ____________ in Italy?
B We ate spaghetti and lasagne.

17 SPEAKING **Work in pairs. Write questions to ask your partner about their last holiday. Then ask and answer.**

... go? *... stay?* *... do?* *... a good time?*
... photos? *... on your own?*

→ workbook page 101

PRONUNCIATION
Past simple irregular verbs Go to page 121.

READING

1 **Look at the pictures. These animals don't exist today: they are extinct. Match them with the names in the article. Write 1–3 in the boxes.**

2 11.05 **Read and listen to the article. Check your answers.**

EXTINCT ANIMALS

A ☐

B ☐

C ☐

1 THE GREAT AUK

The great auk was a large seabird that lived in the North Atlantic. It was a bird, but it couldn't fly. It could swim under water really well. It caught and ate fish when it dived under the water. Its feathers were very soft and people used them to make pillows for their beds. Because of this, people killed the birds. The last great auk died on the island of Eldey in 1835.

2 THE TASMANIAN TIGER

The Tasmanian tiger was only found in Australia, Tasmania and New Guinea. It got its name because it had stripes like a tiger, but it was not a member of the cat family. Farmers believed Tasmanian tigers killed their sheep, so they paid people to kill them. Many of the tigers died after getting ill from diseases they caught from other animals. The last Tasmanian tiger died in Hobart Zoo in 1936.

3 STELLER'S SEA COW

Steller's sea cow was a large animal that lived in the cold Arctic waters around Alaska. It grew up to nine metres long. Because it was so big, it couldn't go under the water. It ate the plants on top of the sea. It wasn't a very dangerous animal – it was quite friendly. Because of this, it was very easy to kill. Europeans first found the sea cow in 1741. 27 years later they killed the last one.

3 **Read the article again. Write the names of the animals.**

0 This animal was a bird, but it couldn't fly. *great auk*
1 This animal was the last to go. ______
2 Farmers didn't like this animal. ______
3 This animal lived in the sea, but couldn't go under the water. ______
4 People killed this bird for its feathers. ______
5 This animal was not afraid of humans. ______

4 SPEAKING **Do you know any other animals that are extinct? Talk to your partner.**

GRAMMAR
could / couldn't (ability)

5 Complete the examples from the article on page 106. Then read the rule.

1 It ___________ swim under water really well.

2 It was so big, it ___________ go under the water.

RULE: We use *could / couldn't* + the base form of a verb to talk about ability in the past.

6 Use *could/couldn't* and a verb from the list to complete the sentences.

~~do~~ | drive | play | ride | see | speak

0 The homework last night was very difficult. *I couldn't do* it! ✗

1 My grandmother ___________ without her glasses. ✗

2 My brother ___________ the guitar when he was only seven. ✓

3 I ___________ a bicycle when I was four. ✓

4 My dad ___________ a car until he was 25. ✗

5 My grandfather was amazing; he ___________ five languages. ✓

7 SPEAKING Work in pairs. Think about what you could or couldn't do when you were five. Use the ideas in the list. Add your own ideas.

cook	speak English
dance	swim
read and write	take photos
ride a bicycle	use a tablet

When I was five, I couldn't ride a bicycle.

When I was five, I could swim.

→ workbook page 101

VOCABULARY
Adjectives

8 11.06 Write the words in the list under the photos. There are six extra words you don't need. Listen and check.

beautiful | boring | clean | clever | dangerous | dirty
horrible | interesting | lovely | safe | stupid | ugly

1 ___________

4 ___________

2 ___________

5 ___________

3 ___________

6 ___________

9 SPEAKING Work in pairs or in small groups. Use the adjectives from Exercise 8 to talk about these things.

a famous person | a sport you like
a TV programme | your town

I think our town is ugly.

Really? I think it's beautiful.

10 Match the adjectives and their opposites from Exercise 8.

→ workbook page 102

WRITING
An extinct animal

11 Choose an animal that is extinct. Try and find the answers to these questions.

1 What kind of animal was it?

2 Where did it live?

3 What did it look like?

4 What could it do/not do?

5 Why did it die out?

12 SPEAKING Work in pairs. Tell your partner about your animal.

13 Use your answers from Exercise 11 to write a short text (60–90 words) about the animal.

DEVELOPING SPEAKING

1 **Look at the photo. Where is the boy?**

2 11.07 **Now read and listen to the dialogue. Who's afraid of snakes?**

Lena: Hey Nathan. How are you? Did you have a good weekend?
Nathan: Well, sort of. I mean … it was OK.
Lena: You don't sound very sure! What happened?
Toby: Yeah, come on, tell us.
Nathan: All right. Well, on Sundays we usually go for a walk, my family and I. But yesterday, I went alone.
Toby: Where did you go?
Nathan: I went to the forest – you know, outside town. It's really nice there. And I started walking, when suddenly …
Lena: Yes? Suddenly what?
Nathan: Well, in front of me, there was a snake.
Toby: Are there snakes in the forest? Are you sure?
Nathan: Yes, I'm sure. It was on the path. I stopped. I didn't do anything. Then it just went away. I was afraid.
Lena: Poor you! I hate snakes, too.
Toby: Why were you afraid? It's just a snake. A snake can't kill you.
Lena: Some snakes can! Anyway, it's OK to be afraid sometimes.
Nathan: Thanks, Lena. Anyway, that's why my weekend was just OK.

3 SPEAKING **Read the dialogue again. Answer the questions with a partner.**

1 What was different about Nathan's walk this Sunday?
2 What did he see in front of him?
3 What did he do?
4 Who thinks it was OK for Nathan to be afraid?

Phrases for fluency

4 **Find the expressions 1–4 in the dialogue. Who says them? How do you say them in your language?**

1 What happened? ________
2 All right. ________
3 suddenly … ________
4 Poor you! ________

5 **Put the sentences in the correct order to make a dialogue.**

☐ **Gio** It's true. I was so afraid I jumped on the chair and fell off!
☐ **Gio** Because I saw a big, horrible spider!
1 **Gio** Can I tell you what happened yesterday?
☐ **Gio** I was in the kitchen, and suddenly, I fell off my chair.
☐ **Natalie** What? You saw a spider and fell off your chair?
☐ **Natalie** All right. What happened?
☐ **Natalie** Oh, poor you! But why?

6 **Complete the dialogues with the expressions from Exercise 4.**

0 A You look really happy! *What happened?*
B I got my test results. 95%!
1 A I think I'm ill.
B ______________ ! Perhaps you should stay in bed today.
2 A Dad was horrible last night.
B I know. At first he was OK, but ______________ he got angry!
3 A There's a great new online computer game. Can I play it, Dad?
B ______________ , but only for half an hour. You've got homework.

FUNCTIONS
Sequencing (in a story)

KEY LANGUAGE
First, …
Then …
After that, …
Later, …
Finally … / In the end, …

7 **What did Jake do yesterday? Choose the correct word for every sentence.**

[1]*After that / First*, Jake got up and had a shower. [2]*Then / In the end*, he had breakfast and did his homework. [3]*After that / Finally*, he went to his grandma's house for lunch. [4]*In the end / Later*, he went to the cinema with his friend Bruno. [5]*Finally / First*, he went to bed.

8 **Think of a story to tell a partner. Use one of the ideas below or your own idea. Make notes.**

- what you did last weekend
- what you did on your last birthday
- something funny that happened to you

9 SPEAKING **Tell your partner your story. Use the sequencing words from the Key Language box to structure your story.**

LIFE COMPETENCIES

Everyone is scared of something – a person, a thing or a situation at some time in their life. By being positive and trying new things, we can face our fear and even beat it!

1 ▶33 **Watch the vlog. Tick (✓) the things Ethan is scared of.**

A

C

B

D

E

2 ▶33 **Watch the vlog again. What advice can you give Ethan?**

3 **Read the dialogues. What are Tom, Nadia and Lara afraid of?**

1 **Harry** Come on, I don't want to walk up the stairs to the fifth floor.
Tom Sorry, no. I can't get into a lift, no way.
Harry Why? Did something happen to you?
Tom Yes. When I was only six, I got stuck in a lift for 20 minutes! It was awful. I was so scared.
Harry Oh, poor you. But look, it's only five floors and it's only you and me here. I can help you and talk to you.
Tom OK. Yes, I'll try. Here's the lift now. Let's go in.

2 **Nadia** Look, there's that boy, Alex. He's so nice.
Sadie Yes, he's a nice guy – and I know you like him. So, go and say hello. Talk to him.
Nadia No, I can't do that! I'm too scared.
Sadie Scared of what? You're nice, too – I'm sure he likes you.
Nadia But …
Sadie No buts. Come on, let's go and say hi.

3 **Lara** This is great. I love running! Oh, wait! Oh, no!
Grace What's the matter, Lara? Are you tired?
Lara No, that's not it. Look, there's a dog over there. I'm scared.
Grace Of that little dog? It can't hurt you! It's asleep. And it's really small, too.
Lara But I'm really scared of dogs, Grace. Can we turn round and run back now, please?
Grace Oh, Lara, don't be silly! Come on.

4 SPEAKING **Ask and answer the questions with a partner.**

1 Why is Tom scared of lifts?
2 How does Harry help Tom?
3 Why do you think Nadia is scared of talking to Alex?
4 What does Grace say that isn't supportive?

Me and my world

5 **Make a list of things that people are often scared of.**

6 SPEAKING **Work in pairs. Are you scared of any of the things on your lists? What can people do to not be afraid?**

TIPS FOR FACING OUR FEARS

- Remember that everybody is afraid of something.
- Remember that it is often possible to stop feeling afraid of something.
- You shouldn't stop doing the things you want to do.

12 MOVING ABOUT

OBJECTIVES

FUNCTIONS: talking about travel and transport; comparing things; at the train station

GRAMMAR: comparative adjectives; *one* / *ones*

VOCABULARY: transport; geographical places

Get THINKING

Watch the video and think: what kinds of transport do you use?

READING

1 **Match the words in the list with the photos. Write 1–5 in the boxes.**

1 a bike | 2 a boat | 3 a bus | 4 a car | 5 an underground train

2 SPEAKING **Work in pairs. When do you use the types of transport in Exercise 1?**

I go to my friend's house by bike.

I go to school by bus.

3 **Put the types of transport in Exercise 1 in order of speed: 1 = slow, 5 = fast.**

4 12.01 **Read and listen to the article and write the type of transport under each medal.**

1 ______ 2 ______ 3 ______ 4 ______

5 **Read the article again and match the questions with the answers.**

0 Why did the TV show presenters have a race? *d*

1 Why did they choose different types of transport?

2 Why was there a surprise?

3 Why weren't the presenters happy?

4 What did the presenters say about the bike?

5 Why is the bike good to use in a city?

a To find the best one.

b Because they wanted the car to win.

c Because it is cheap, clean and healthy.

d To find the best way to get across London.

e It was dangerous.

f Because the bike won.

GRAMMAR
one / ones

4 **Look at the examples from the article on page 114. What do the words *one* and *ones* refer to? Then complete the rule with *plural* and *singular*.**

1 I really love steam trains. There's one in Scotland.

2 I love looking for birds. There are some lovely ones.

RULE: To avoid repeating a noun, we often use *one* in place of [3]__________ nouns and *ones* in place of [4]__________ nouns.

5 **Write *one* or *ones* in the spaces to replace the crossed out words.**

0 A Do you want to watch this film?
B No, I've seen that ~~film~~ ___*one*___ before.

1 A Do you want to try on these jeans?
B No, I'd like to try on the ~~jeans~~ __________ behind them.

2 A What bus can we take?
B Any ~~bus~~ __________ that's got 'City centre' on the front of it.

3 I've got three children. The oldest ~~child~~ __________ is a boy and the younger ~~children~~ __________ are girls.

4 There's a bank in the High Street and there's another ~~bank~~ __________ in Foregate Street.

5 I've got lots of books, but my favourite ~~books~~ __________ are my bird books.

→ workbook page 109

VOCABULARY
Geographical places

6 **Complete the words with the first and last letters. Use the article on page 114 to help you.**

0 m <u>o u n t a i</u> n

1 _ e a c _

2 _ i v e _

3 _ e _

4 _ i e l _

5 _ a k _

6 _ a r _

7 _ o r e s _

7 SPEAKING **Work in pairs. Make a list of famous …**

a beaches
b rivers
c seas
d lakes

8 **Think about your favourite journey. Make notes.**

Where to	
How	
Who with	

9 SPEAKING **Tell your partner about your journey.**

My favourite journey is to the mountains to go skiing.

How do you get there?

We go by car.

→ workbook page 110

TH!NK

Transport around the world

Culture

TRANSPORT AROUND THE WORLD

1 ________________

3 ________________

2 ________________

4 ________________

THE AMFIBUS, THE NETHERLANDS

The big, blue Amfibus certainly makes a big splash! It's in Rotterdam and it takes people on tours of the city. It's cool. It can travel on land and in the water. It is more expensive than water taxis, but it is more exciting, too. It is slower in the water than on land. It goes at 8kmph in the water and 96kmph on land. The tour lasts for an hour and it costs 27.50 euros.

MOVING WALKWAYS AND ESCALATORS, HONG KONG

The Central-Mid-Levels Escalator is 800 metres long. Escalators are usually inside a shopping centre or an airport, but not this one! It's outside. It's a great way to travel round this city of hills. And it's free! There are 14 places where you can get on and off. The escalators travel down the hill from 6am to 10am so people can travel to work. They travel up the hill from 10am to midnight.

THE URBAN CABLE CAR, TURKEY

Ankara's cable car is cheaper than other forms of public transport and it is healthier because it doesn't pollute the air. It is also easier and quicker than travelling by car because there are no traffic jams in the sky! It travels 60 metres above the ground and passengers can get great views of the city.

SUBMARINES, LANZAROTE AND TENERIFE

Now you can travel in a submarine! This submarine carries tourists. It is a safe and comfortable way to see the colourful fish and the plants and rocks under our seas. The submarine can carry 48 people and it has 11 large windows on each side. It travels down 60 metres under the sea.

1 **Look at the photos on page 116. Find these things.**

a bus | a cable car | a city | an escalator | a submarine | water

2 12.07 **Read and listen to the article. Write the name of the transport under the photos.**

3 **Read the article again and tick (✓) the correct boxes.**

	the Amfibus	urban cable car	escalator	submarine
1 You have a great view of the city.	☐	☐	☐	☐
2 You often see these in a shopping centre or an airport.	☐	☐	☐	☐
3 It travels on water and on land.	☐	☐	☐	☐
4 It is a quicker way to travel than by car.	☐	☐	☐	☐
5 It's a safe and comfortable way to travel under water.	☐	☐	☐	☐

4 SPEAKING **Discuss these questions with a partner.**

1 Which of these types of transport would you most like to travel on?
2 Are there any unusual types of transport in your country? Where?

WRITING
Unusual forms of transport

1 INPUT **Read the text. What's the name of the transport?**

2 ANALYSE **Read the text again and answer the questions.**

1 Where can you see it?
2 What type of transport is it?
3 Why is it unusual?

3 PLAN **Choose one of these unusual types of transport or one that you already know about. Look on the internet for information. Make notes to answer the questions in Exercise 2.**

The Chiva bus, Colombia
The Coco Taxi, Cuba
The Hovercraft, Isle of Wight, UK

4 PRODUCE **Use your notes to write a short text about your form of transport from Exercise 3. Write 60–100 words.**

THE ICE ANGEL IN WISCONSIN

Wisconsin is a state in the US. There are large lakes in Wisconsin. One of the lakes is called Lake Superior. In winter, it is very cold and the water in the lake turns to ice. When the ice is hard, cars can drive across it. But sometimes the ice is very thin. Then, only the Ice Angel can cross it. The Ice Angel is a very special bus. It can travel on water, snow and ice. In summer, it travels on water, and in winter, it travels across the ice. It takes people from Wisconsin's Madeline Island to Bayfield.

TOWARDS A2 Key for Schools

READING AND WRITING
Short message

1 **You want to go out and have lunch with your English friend Reese on Sunday. Write an email to Reese.**

In the email:

- ask Reese to go out for lunch with you on Sunday
- say where you would like to go for lunch
- say what you would like to eat.

Write 25 words or more.

Part 7: Picture story

2 **Look at the three pictures. Write the story shown in the pictures. Write 35 words or more.**

LISTENING
3-option multiple choice

3 12.08 **Listen to Polly talking to her friend Seth about their pets. For each question choose the right answer (A, B or C).**

1 Spot is
   A Polly's dog. B Seth's dog. C Seth's mum's dog.

2 Flopsie is a
   A rabbit. B cat. C dog.

3 Polly's pet is a
   A rabbit called Nemo. B fish called Nemo. C cat called Nemo.

4 Nemo eats once a
   A day. B week. C month.

5 Polly cleans Nemo's bowl
   A every week. B three times a week. C once a month.

VOCABULARY

1 Complete the sentences with the words in the list. There are two extra words.

did | do | farm | forest | fun | get | go | had | horrible | motorbike | safe | taxi

1 That river is dirty and ugly. I think it's ______________ .
2 Let's have some ______________ this weekend. How about going to the beach?
3 We went to Manchester last weekend and we ______________ a really good time.
4 There are lots of animals on that ______________ .
5 It's snowing! Let's ______________ skiing this afternoon.
6 Dangerous? No, it's very ______________ , I promise.
7 The weekend was really boring. I just ______________ my homework, nothing else.
8 I don't think it's a good idea to ride a ______________ in a big city.
9 It's not a big deal. Please don't ______________ angry about it.
10 We missed the last bus so we took a ______________ to get home.

/10

GRAMMAR

2 Complete the sentences with the words in the list.

better | couldn't | did | good | more | ones | went

1 I was ill, so I ______________ go to your party, sorry.
2 Green? No thanks, I like the blue ______________ over there.
3 I love that film. It's really ______________ .
4 ______________ you have fun at the party?
5 My new phone was ______________ expensive than my old one.
6 This song is ______________ than the last one.
7 I couldn't go to the concert, but my friends ______________ .

3 Find and correct the mistake in each sentence.

1 Are these your new shoes, or are they the old one?
2 My parents gived me this book for my birthday.
3 The chicken was horrible so I not eat it.
4 Went you to the beach last weekend?
5 I like these jeans because they're cheaper as the other ones.
6 I'm bad at Physics, but Jack is more bad!
7 Did you saw any good films last week?

/14

FUNCTIONAL LANGUAGE

4 Complete the missing words.

1 A Hi. Can I have a t _ _ _ _ _ to Manchester, please?
B OK. S _ _ _ _ _ _ or r _ _ _ _ _ _ ?
2 A What time is the n _ _ _ train to Birmingham, please?
B 3.00 – and after that, there's a train at 3.45.
A OK. I want the 3.00 train. What platform does it l _ _ _ _ from?
B Platform 4. Have a good j _ _ _ _ _ _ _ !

/6

MY SCORE /30

22–30 | 10–21 | 0–9

PRONUNCIATION

UNIT 1

/h/ or /w/ in question words

1 1.03 **Read and listen to the questions.**

How old are you?
Where are you from?
What's your favourite food?
Who's your favourite football player?
Why do you like him?

2 **Say the question words in blue.**

3 1.04 **Listen again and repeat. Then practise with a partner.**

UNIT 2

Vowel sounds – adjectives

1 2.03 **Read and listen to the dialogue.**

Tom	Mum's hungry.
Jane	Mum? But why? Why is she angry?
Tom	I said Mum's hungry. She wants a sandwich.
Jane	Oh … OK. Well, Dad's angry.
Tom	Does he want a sandwich, too?
Jane	No! I said he's angry.

2 **Which sounds are different in *hungry* and *angry*? Say them and make the differences clear.**

3 2.04 **Listen again and repeat. Then practise with a partner.**

UNIT 3

this / that / these / those

1 3.05 **Read and listen to the dialogue.**

Anna	Can I have that cake, please?
Assistant	This one or that one?
Anna	That one – the chocolate one.
Assistant	That's a fruitcake, but these cupcakes are chocolate.
Anna	Oh! Can I have two of those, then?
Assistant	Of course. Here you are.

2 **Say the words *that, this, those* and *these*.**

3 3.06 **Listen again and repeat. Then practise with a partner.**

UNIT 4

Word stress in numbers

1 4.07 **Read and listen to the dialogue.**

Tim	It's my sister's birthday today. She's thirteen.
Julie	Thirty! That's old!
Tim	Thirty? No! I said, 'Thirteen'.
Julie	Oh … thirteen. She's the same age as me.

2 **Where is the stress on the red words? Where is the stress on the blue words?**

3 4.08 **Listen again and repeat. Then practise with a partner.**

UNIT 5

Present simple verbs – third person

1 5.02 **Read and listen to the sentences.**

Liz catches the bus to school every morning.
She teaches French at a secondary school.
At 4.30, she finishes work.
After dinner, Liz washes the dishes.
Before she goes to bed, she chooses her clothes for the next day.

2 **How many syllables are there in *catch*? How many syllables are there in *catches*? Say the words in blue.**

3 5.03 **Listen again and repeat. Then practise with a partner.**

UNIT 6

Long vowel sound /eɪ/

1 6.05 **Read and listen to the dialogue.**

Customer	I'm sorry I'm late. I have a table for 1.00.
Server	That's okay. But Jane Grey's waiting for you.
Customer	OK. But I don't know her. Is she the girl there, with the long straight hair?
Server	No. Her hair's wavy and grey.
Customer	Oh! The woman with the pink face? The one eating cake?
Server	Yes, that's her. I'll take you to the table.

2 **Say the words in blue. Which vowel sound do they all have?**

3 6.06 **Listen again and repeat. Then practise with a partner.**

UNIT 7

Long vowel sound /ɔː/

1 7.02 **Read and listen to the dialogue.**

Paul Do you like sport?
Laura Oh, yes, it's very important. I love skateboarding.
Paul So do I! Are there any more sports you like?
Laura Well, I like all ball games. Hmm … what time is it, Paul?
Paul It's quarter to four, Laura.
Laura I have to go. I'm playing football at four.

2 **Say the words in blue. Which vowel sound do they all have?**

3 7.03 **Listen again and repeat. Then practise with a partner.**

UNIT 8

Intonation – listing items

1 8.05 **Read and listen to the dialogue.**

Mum I'm going shopping. Do you want anything?
Brad Yes, Mum! I need a T-shirt. Oh, and some socks, please.
Mum OK. A T-shirt and socks …
Brad Actually, I need a T-shirt ↑↓, socks ↑↓, trainers ↑↓, a jacket ↑↓ and a baseball ↑↓ cap.
Mum A T-shirt, socks, trainers, a jacket and a baseball cap. I think you need to come with me!

2 **Brad wants *a T-shirt, socks, trainers, a jacket* and *a baseball cap*. Circle the arrows to show when his voice goes up and when it goes down.**

3 8.06 **Listen again and repeat. Then practise with a partner.**

UNIT 9

Intonation – giving two choices

1 9.06 **Read and listen to the dialogue.**

Server Would you like salad ↑↓ or soup ↑↓?
Mike Salad, please.
Server Chicken ↑↓ or fish ↑↓?
Mike I think I'll have fish today.
Server Would you like dessert?
Mike Yes, please!
Server Cake ↑↓ or fruit ↑↓?
Mike Hmm … I'll have the fruit.
Server And coffee ↑↓ or tea ↑↓?
Mike Oh, coffee, please.

2 9.07 **Circle the arrows in the dialogue to show when the server's voice goes up and when it goes down. Listen and check.**

3 9.07 **Listen again and repeat. Then practise with a partner.**

UNIT 10

Past simple regular verbs

1 10.06 **Read and listen to the story.**

My grandmother lived in the country. She walked to town to go to school. She started working in a bottle factory. She worked in the factory until she married my grandfather. One day, she invented a machine that cleaned bottles. The factory wanted the machine and my grandparents were rich after that!

2 **The *-ed* ending is pronounced differently in the red and blue words. What's the difference?**

3 10.07 **Listen again and repeat. Then practise with a partner.**

UNIT 11

Past simple irregular verbs

1 11.03 **Read and listen to the dialogue.**

Peter Could you ride a bike when you were young, Grandma?
Grandma I certainly could, Peter. I went to school on my bike. I put my books in the basket.
Peter Could you swim?
Grandma Of course I could! One day I swam across the lake near my house.

2 **Say the past tense words in blue. What is the infinitive form of these verbs?**

3 11.04 **Listen again and repeat. Then practise with a partner.**

UNIT 12

Word stress – comparatives

1 12.03 **Read and listen to the sentences.**

A plane is faster than a car.
A bike is slower than a train.
A speedboat is quicker than a ferry.

2 **Find the comparative adjective in each sentence. Which syllable is stressed in each of these words?**

3 12.04 **Listen again and repeat. Then practise with a partner.**

GET IT RIGHT!

UNIT 1

To be

Learners often miss out *am*, *are* or *is* in sentences.
We use the subject + *be* + object.
✓ *I'm from Spain.*
✗ *~~I from Spain.~~*

In questions, we use *be* + subject + object + question mark.
✓ *Are they from Scotland?*
✗ *~~They from Scotland?~~*

Tick (✓) the correct sentences and cross (✗) the incorrect ones. Correct the mistakes.

0 He my favourite athlete. ✗
He is my favourite athlete.
1 The house very nice. ☐
2 How old you? ☐
3 I'm from Edinburgh. ☐
4 You 13 years old? ☐
5 What your name? ☐
6 My favourite singer is Sam Smith. ☐
7 My name John. ☐
8 Lisbon in Spain? ☐

Subject pronouns and *to be*

Learners sometimes miss out the subject pronoun when using *be*.
We always use the subject + *be*.
✓ *This is Mike. He is from England.*
✗ *This is Mike. ~~Is from England.~~*

Correct the mistakes in the sentences.

0 I like Maria. Is very funny.
I like Maria. She is very funny.
1 I like England. Is very nice.
2 It's a taxi. Is yellow.
3 She's my friend. Is from Mexico.
4 They are singers. Are in Little Mix.
5 He's my brother. Is 15 years old.
6 I like this phone because is very small.

UNIT 2

To be questions

Learners make mistakes with word order in *be* questions.
In positive sentences, we use subject + *be*.
In questions, we use the order *be* + subject + (object) followed with a question mark (?).
✓ *That is OK.*
✓ *Is that OK?*
✗ *~~That is OK?~~*

Put the words in the correct order to make questions.

0 it / expensive / is ?
Is it expensive?
1 there / is / problem / a ?
2 on / holiday / are / you ?
3 how / you / are ?
4 a / is / famous person / he ?
5 computer game / this / is / your ?
6 she / is / sister / your ?

Spelling

Learners sometimes have trouble spelling words in English.
✓ *That is my pencil.*
✗ *That is my ~~pensil~~.*

Correct the spelling mistakes in the sentences.

0 She is my frind.
She is my friend.
1 My brother is very funy.
2 The food is excelent.
3 My shirt is withe.
4 We play football in the evining.
5 I saw her yesterday moring.
6 The film is greate.

UNIT 3

Possessive 's

Learners find it difficult to use possessive *'s*. They often put the words in the wrong order.
We use person + possessive *'s* + thing/person.
✓ *This is my brother's car.*
✗ *This is ~~the car of my brother~~.*

Rewrite the sentences using possessive *'s*.

0 I went to the house of my cousin.
I went to my cousin's house.
1 It is the homework of my sister.
2 The name of my friend is Amy.
3 I was at the party of my friend.
4 The family of my friend lives in India.
5 It is the birthday of my sister.
6 This is the bedroom of my brother.
7 Trumpington High is the school of my cousin.
8 Don't eat the burger of Juan!
9 That's the chair of the teacher.
10 He's the brother of Ana.

Family vocabulary

Learners sometimes make spelling mistakes with family words.
✓ *This is my cousin Jean.*
✗ *This is my ~~cousine~~ Jean.*
✗ *This is my ~~couzin~~ Jean.*

Correct the spelling mistakes in the family words.

0 How is your familly?
How is your family?
1 My mather is in hospital.
2 We go to my granmother's house.
3 I watch films with my borther.
4 It was a present from my fater.
5 He is the president's sun.
6 He has got two daugthers.
7 My granfather lives there.
8 She is my cousine.
9 Does your uncel live near you?

UNIT 4

There is / There are

Learners sometimes miss out *there* where *there is/are* is required.
We use *there* + *be* + noun, where *be* agrees with the noun. We do not use *there have* or *there has*.
✓ *There is a great café on this street.*
✗ *~~Is a great café~~ on this street.*
✗ *~~There has a great café~~ on this street.*

Correct the mistakes in the sentences.

0 Next week is a party.
Next week there is a party.
1 In the kitchen are two windows.
2 In Paris there has a nice park.
3 Are any other drinks?
4 In my room there has a bed.
5 It is nice because are lots of shops.
6 Near my town there have lots of interesting places.

Prepositions of place

Learners sometimes make mistakes with the form of prepositions of place, either misspelling them or using the wrong particle.
✓ *The shop is next to the post office.*
✗ *The shop is ~~next the post office.~~*

Correct the mistakes in the sentences.

0 My house is oposite the school.
My house is opposite the school.
1 The coffee shop is infront of the bank.
2 My house is nex to Park Hotel.
3 I live behing the station.
4 Station Road is beetween the supermarket and the post office.
5 The shop is opposit the museum.
6 Their houses are next the hospital.

UNIT 5

Present simple positive

Learners often make agreement mistakes in the present simple.

✓ *It helps me with my studies.*

✗ *It ~~help~~ me with my studies.*

Correct the mistakes in the sentences.

0 He play football.

He plays football.

1 He eat breakfast every day.

2 They likes sports.

3 She go to university.

4 Angela work Monday to Friday.

5 People plays games on their phones.

6 School start on Friday.

7 People in cities is often angry.

8 He studyies every day after school.

9 She love Glee Club.

10 My brother watchs football on TV every Saturday.

Present simple negative

Learners sometimes make agreement mistakes in the present simple negative.

The verb *do* agrees with the person and number of the subject.

✓ *He doesn't like sports.*

✗ *He ~~don't~~ like sports.*

Choose the correct options in the sentences.

0 They *don't* / *doesn't* understand.

1 She *doesn't* / *don't* have any time.

2 He *doesn't* / *don't* like sweets.

3 We *doesn't* / *don't* need to wear tennis clothes.

4 It *don't* / *doesn't* cost much.

5 My teacher *don't* / *doesn't* give me a lot of homework.

6 I *don't* / *doesn't* like computer games.

7 I *don't* / *doesn't* play sports after school.

8 You *don't* / *doesn't* go to my school.

9 My brother *don't* / *doesn't* help me with my homework.

10 Planes *don't* / *doesn't* fly to our city.

UNIT 6

Countable and uncountable nouns

Learners sometimes confuse *a(n)* with *some*.

We use *a* or *an* with countable nouns in the singular.

We use *some* for countable nouns in the plural.

✓ *We can buy a present for his birthday.*

✗ *We can buy ~~some present~~ for his birthday.*

✓ *We can buy some presents for his birthday.*

We also use *some* with uncountable nouns.

✓ *You need some water.*

✗ *You need ~~a water~~.*

Choose the correct options in the sentences.

0 I've got *some* / *a* T-shirt.

1 We took a break and ate *some* / *a* sandwich.

2 The best present was *some* / *a* jacket.

3 I have got *some* / *a* good news.

4 Can you take *some* / *a* photo of us?

5 I often listen to *some* / *a* nice music with my family.

6 He has got *some* / *a* good friends.

has / have got

Learners often forget to include *got* when they use *has / have got* in negative sentences and questions.

✓ *Has he got a dog?*

✗ *~~Has~~ he a dog?*

✓ *He hasn't got a bike.*

✗ *He ~~hasn't~~ a bike.*

Correct the mistakes in the sentences.

0 I haven't any sisters.

I haven't got any sisters.

1 Have you the time?

2 Has your mum GPS in her car?

3 I haven't headphones. Can I use yours?

4 They haven't books in their school. They use tablets.

5 I haven't an e-reader. I use my phone.

6 Have you a laptop?

UNIT 7
can / can't

Learners sometimes use the wrong form of the verb when they use *can* and *to*.
We use the infinitive without *to* after *can*.
✓ *He can play the piano.*
✗ *He ~~can to play~~ the piano.*

We use *to* + infinitive after *want* and *need*.
✓ *They want to know the answer.*
✗ *They ~~want know~~ the answer.*

Correct the mistakes in the sentences.

0 He needs do that.
He needs to do that.
1 Can you to speak Spanish?
2 We want do some shopping.
3 You need clean your room.
4 I need eat something. I'm hungry!
5 I can't to do my homework.
6 Alex wants do everything.

UNIT 8
like / don't like + verb + *-ing*

Learners sometimes use the wrong form of the verb where *-ing* is required.
We use the *-ing* form of verbs after the verbs *like*, *don't like*, *love* and *hate*.
✓ *I like playing tennis.*
✗ *I ~~like play~~ tennis.*
✗ *I ~~like to playing~~ tennis.*

Correct the mistakes in the sentences.

0 I like read books.
I like reading books.
1 I like sing and dancing.
2 We love go shopping.
3 She likes to wearing green clothes.
4 They don't like play basketball.
5 Paul doesn't hate study.
6 Anna likes to wearing white clothes.

UNIT 9
must / mustn't / can / would

Learners often have trouble spelling modal verbs *can't*, *must*, *would* and *mustn't*.

Correct the spelling mistakes in the sentences.

0 Wold you like to go with me?
Would you like to go with me?
1 I cant find the coffee.
2 You mast learn English.
3 I woud like to do some shopping.
4 You musn't use YouTube©.
5 Woudn't you like some more?
6 We mussn't be late.

UNIT 10
was / wasn't, were / weren't

Learners sometimes confuse *was* and *were*.
***Was*, *wasn't*, *were* and *weren't* all have to agree with the subject.**
✓ *The jeans were very beautiful.*
✗ *The jeans ~~was~~ very beautiful.*

Tick (✓) the correct sentences and cross (✗) the incorrect ones. Correct the mistakes.

0 There was a lot of people. [✗]
There were a lot of people.
1 We was at Dan's house all night. [ ]
2 There was a lot of food. [ ]
3 Wasn't you there? [ ]
4 I were happy to see you at the weekend. [ ]
5 How many people were at your house? [ ]
6 Last night there were a party on the beach. [ ]
7 He was my friend at school. [ ]
8 Katie and Jo was there. [ ]

UNIT 11

Past simple (irregular verbs)

Learners sometimes use the wrong forms of irregular verbs in the past simple or misspell them.

✓ *I paid a lot of money.*

✗ *I ~~payed~~ a lot of money.*

Correct the mistakes in the sentences.

0 I haved a holiday.
I had a holiday.
1 I maked a lot of friends.
2 She gived me a lot of presents.
3 Jack and Al taked photographs.
4 There where some problems with his work.
5 I cam home late yesterday.
6 He swimmed very fast.
7 They goed to the cinema.
8 Helen mad some food.

Past simple (negative)

Learners sometimes use the present simple negative where the past simple is required.

✓ *I didn't find the answer before the end of the exam.*

✗ *I ~~don't~~ find the answer before the end of the exam.*

Choose the correct options.

0 We *don't* / *(didn't)* go to the game last week.
1 I *didn't* / *don't* need any help at the moment.
2 I bought some T-shirts but I *didn't* / *don't* buy any tops.
3 I went to a mobile phone shop but I *didn't* / *don't* like the phones there.
4 Do you like chicken? No, I *didn't* / *don't* eat meat.
5 I had a lot of presents but he *didn't* / *don't* give me one.
6 We *didn't* / *don't* usually go on holiday because we like being at home.

UNIT 12

Comparative adjectives

Learners often use *more* and *-er* in the same sentence when only one of these forms is required.
We form comparative adjectives by adding *-er* if the adjective has one syllable (or two syllables ending in *-y*), and by using *more* if the adjective has two or more syllables. We don't use *more* and *-er* together.

✓ *This one is bigger than that one.*

✗ *This one is ~~more bigger~~ than that one.*

✗ *This one is ~~more big~~ than that one.*

Correct the mistakes in the sentences.

0 The train is more cheap than the plane.
The train is cheaper than the plane.
1 He is more healthier than he was last year.
2 Henry is more older than his brother.
3 My mobile phone is more newer than my brother's.
4 Basketball is more good than baseball.
5 I was more happy than Joe at the end of the game.
6 Henry's brother is more friendlier than Henry.
7 I think Maths is more easy than English.

than with comparative adjectives

Learners sometimes use *then* or *that* where *than* is required with comparative adjectives.

✓ *Colin is older than Oliver.*

✗ *Colin is older ~~then~~ Oliver.*

✗ *Colin is older ~~that~~ Oliver.*

Complete the sentences with *then*, *that* or *than*.

0 He can run faster ___*than*___ me.
1 It is much better ____________ your mobile phone.
2 Call me ____________ .
3 It is more ____________ I thought.
4 ____________ is my book.
5 This one is better than ____________ one.
6 We danced and ____________ watched a film.

STUDENT A

UNIT 4, PAGE 43, VOCABULARY

Student A
Ask and answer the questions with your partner.

How much is the smartphone? *It's ...*

How much are the ...? *They're ...*

UNIT 6, PAGE 61, TRAIN TO THINK

Student A
Describe to your partner what the people in your picture look like. Your partner describes what the people in his/her picture look like. Find the six differences.

UNIT 8, PAGE 79, TRAIN TO THINK

Student A
Listen to the questions your partner asks about the picture in Exercise 2. Answer with short answers. Correct the negative answers.

1 Are there ten people in the band?
2 Is the singer wearing a red dress?
3 Are there two guitar players in the band?
4 Are there five trumpet players in the band?
5 Are all the band members wearing hats?

STUDENT B

UNIT 4, PAGE 43, VOCABULARY

Student B
Ask and answer the questions with your partner.

How much is the TV?

It's …

How much are the …?

They're …

UNIT 6, PAGE 61, TRAIN TO THINK

Student B
Describe to your partner what the people in your picture look like. Your partner describes what the people in his/her picture look like. Find the six differences.

UNIT 8, PAGE 79, TRAIN TO THINK

Student B
Listen to the questions your partner asks about the picture in Exercise 2. Answer with short answers. Correct the negative answers.

1 Are there eight people dancing?
2 Are the two dancing women wearing green dresses?
3 Is one dancing man wearing a blue shirt?
4 Are eight people drinking?
5 Are four people sitting down?